The Gen X Series

MATHS OLYMPIAD 2

Useful for Maths Olympiads Conducted at School, National & International Levels

Author
Shraddha Singh

Peer Reviewer
Nisha Dhiman

Strictly According to the Latest Syllabus of Maths Olympiad

V&S PUBLISHERS

Published by:

V&S PUBLISHERS

F-2/16, Ansari road, Daryaganj, New Delhi-110002
☎ 23240026, 23240027 • *Fax:* 011-23240028
✉ info@vspublishers.com • 🌐 www.vspublishers.com

Online Brandstore: amazon.in/vspublishers

Regional Office : Hyderabad
5-1-707/1, Brij Bhawan (Beside Central Bank of India Lane)
Bank Street, Koti, Hyderabad - 500 095
☎ 040-24737290
✉ vspublishershyd@gmail.com

Follow us on: f t in

BUY OUR BOOKS FROM: AMAZON FLIPKART

© Copyright: **V&S PUBLISHERS**
ISBN 978-93-579405-1-1
New Edition

Publisher's Note

General Trade and Mass Appeal books across various genres have helped **V&S Publishers** to gain widespread popularity. In a short span of 10 years, we have successfully published more than 1000 titles across 9 languages in our 50 subject categories. Being into the publishing business for about 40 years, we have always been a dynamic publishing house, with a massive distribution network, across India; including E-commerce platforms.

Understanding the need of inculcating knowledge and developing a spirit of healthy competition amongst students to make them ready for the world outside schools and colleges; we created Olympiad Series under the **GEN X SERIES Imprint** which, owning to its rich content and unique representation became popular amongst students, in no time. The motivation is not to improve marks in terms of numbers, but is to make sure that the students are already prepared to face competitive environment with respect to college admissions and cracking various entrance examinations, while ensuring their conceptual clarity.

Published for classes 1-10 across subjects English, Mathematics, Science, Computers, General Knowledge, the books are unlike any other in the market and are written in a guidebook pattern and exhaustively include examples and Multiple-Choice Questions.

Here, we present the latest Edition of **MATHS OLYMPIAD CLASS 2.**

Unique Features of the book are as follows:

☞ Authored by Subject Matter Experts' and Peer reviewed by School Principals and HOD's for the respective subjects

☞ Books based on principles of Applied Psychology and Bloom's Taxonomy

☞ Suited for Olympiad Examinations held at School level, National level & International Level irrespective of organizing body.

☞ The only Olympiad Book in India written in Guidebook Pattern with Concise Theory, images and illustrations.

☞ Exhaustively include Examples, MCQs, Subjective Questions, and HOTS with Answer Keys & Solutions.

☞ Multiple Model Papers for thorough practice also given inside the book with solutions.

☞ OMR sheets appended at the end of the book for simulating exam environment.

Besides, we are also planning to launch an App very soon for the Olympiad preparation which further testifies our constant endeavor to keep up with student demands. We have made sure to closely follow syllabus patterns of not only Olympiad conducting bodies but also education boards & organizations like CBSE and NCERT, to make sure that our books prove useful to students; helping them to boost their academic performance in schools as well.

P.S. While every care has been taken to ensure the correctness of the content, if you come across any error, howsoever minor, do not hesitate to discuss with teachers while pointing that out to us in no uncertain terms.

We wish you All the Best!

DISTINCTIVE

01 LEARNING OBJECTIVES

They list the whole chapter as subtopics, helping the teachers to guide children in a step-by-step manner.

02 DID YOU KNOW

Enhance your knowledge by getting acquainted with some amazing facts across various subjects like science, Mathematics and English.

03 MULTIPLE CHOICE QUESTIONS

MCQs act as an excellent learning aid, helping you to understand and work on your mistakes.

04 THINGS TO REMEMBER

A quick recap of the chapter in a summarized format helps in faster revision along with conceptual clarity.

05 HOTS

The High Order Thinking Questions aim to help the student to solve Application-based questions and gain practical understanding of the subject.

FEATURES

SUBJECTIVE QUESTIONS

Help to place the knowledge gained in orderly fashion by using **"WH"** questions, mostly in the form of bullet points.

06

ACHIEVER'S SECTION

Offers a quick revision of the book along with some new facts for the students to discover.

07

A SET OF OMR SHEETS

To allow the student to practice question in an exam-like format which would help them to get the "feel" of how Olympiad exams take place.

08

MODEL TEST PAPERS

Two model test papers are provided at the end of each book, which help the student to test the knowledge which they have gained after thorough reading of all chapters.

09

ANSWER KEY & SOLUTIONS

Detailed Answer Key along with explanations aid the pupil to indentify, understand the mistakes they make during the course of Olympiad preparation.

10

COMPLEMENT SCHOOL SYLLABI

The syllabi across all Olympiad examination closely follow the pattern of academic books. Hence, they not only provide a competitive examination experience, but also help to revise topics for school examinations as well, while strengthening conceptual precision.

ENHANCEMENT OF ANALYTICAL & LOGICAL REASONING

Practicing analytical ability questions, not only helps in developing intellectual ability but also plays a vital role in building critical thinking ability which helps an individual to think about a question or a crisis like situation in day to day life; from all aspects and directions.

Note to Parents

Dear Parents,

Olympiad examinations come with a plethora of advantages. First and foremost among such advantages is the application of knowledge studied, in the form of multiple-choice questions. It helps the child not only to step away from rote learning, but also helps them to exhibit their competencies across various subjects.

In addition to this, Olympiads help the student to understand the importance of revision and practice, and to imbibe upon these practices; which also prove useful in academic performance of the child.

The Olympiads are conducted across multiple subjects, and help the child to recognize their field of interest, thereby encouraging the students to make a career in the field where they can excel the most.

However, cognitive development of a child is not just limited to the four walls of classroom. Following steps can be encouraged by you, to ensure their ward is able to grasp various concepts with ease or lesser difficulty:

☞ **Eat a balanced diet:** Ensure intake of vitamins and minerals to keep you active. Include fruits and super foods like millet in your diet to ensure healthy functioning of organs. Huge intake of junk food should be avoided.

☞ **Indulge in outdoor activities:** Outdoor games break the monotony of life. Play your heart out in greenery to keep yourself alert, active and fit.

☞ **Sleep well:** A sound sleep of 7-8 hours refreshes the brain and makes it ready to understand new topics with more clarity. A sleep derived person faces difficulty in doing even the simplest tasks of day to day life.

☞ **Reduce your Screen time:** More screen time leads to not only weakening of eyesight but decreases concentration span. Regulated Screen time should be encouraged

☞ **Do not hesitate to raise a hand:** Having a doubt in class? Do not hesitate to ask your parents or teachers. This ensures more Conceptual Clarity and hence leads to Application based understanding of various subjects and topics.

☞ **Teach and Learn:** No need to do rote-learning. Once you understand a topic teach or explain it to your friends, siblings and parents. It brings clarity and ensures the child does his revision this way.

☞ **Keep smiling:** A positive attitude promotes a growth mindset and encourages the child to be more inquisitive and try to learn something new, everyday!

HAPPY LEARNING!

Contents

SECTION 1
MATHEMATICAL
REASONING

Number Sense

CHAPTER SUMMARY

Number System

The number system contains ten digits 0, 1, 2, 3, 4, 5, 6, 7, 8 and 9.

Numbers are written using these digits. These digits are called **ones**. The numerals formed by the digits 1, 2, 3, 4, 5, 6, 7, 8 and 9 are known as **Hindu-Arabic Numbers**.

  (i)   10 ones make 1 ten.

  (ii) 10 tens make 1 hundred.

  (iii) 10 hundred make 1 thousand.

Numerals

Numbers can be written by using different symbols. The numbers represented by particular symbols are known as the **digits** of the system.

Number Sense

It refers to a student's abilty to understand and to use the numbers.

Number Names (3-Digit Numbers)

A 3- digit number can be written in hundreds, tens and ones.

For example, 125 – 1 hundred, 2 tens and 5 ones.

Example : Write the number names of the following:

100, 500, 700, 999

Solution:

Number	Number name
100	Hundred
500	Five hundred
700	Seven hundred
999	Nine hundred ninety - nine

Largest and Smallest Numbers

  (i)   Smallest 1- digit number is 1.

  (ii) The largest 1- digit number is 9.

  (iii) The smallest 2- digit number is 10.

  (iv) The largest 2- digit number is 99.

  (v) The smallest 3- digit number is 100.

  (vi) The largest 3- digit number is 999.

Place Value

Place value of a digit depends on its position in the given number. As the digit moves to the left, its value increases.

In a 3 - digit number, there are three places named :

Ones place, Tens place and Hundred place.

Example : Write the place value of each digit in the number 123.

Solution : The place value of each digit in 123 is as follows:

```
1   2   3
|   |   ↓
|   |   Ones place = 3 ones
|   Tens place = 2 tens
Hundreds place = 1 hundred
```

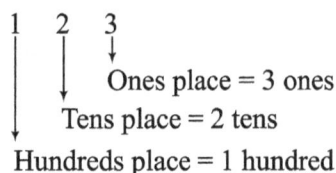

∴ place value of $3 = 3 \times 1 = 3$
place value of $2 = 2 \times 10 = 20$
place value of $1 = 1 \times 100 = 100$

Note : The place value of 0 is always zero.

Expanded Form

Expanded form of 999 is :

$999 = 9$ hundred $+ 9$ tens $+ 9$ ones
$= 900 + 90 + 9$

Ascending Order of Numbers

Arranging the given numbers from smallest to the largest is called **ascending order** or increasing order.

For example : 16, 67, 112, 157 are in ascending order.

Descending Order of Numbers

Arranging the given numbers from largest to the smallest is called **descending order** or decreasing order.

For example : 157, 112, 67, 16 are in descending order.

Comparing the Numbers

We use the following signs to compare the given numbers.

Equal To =

This is the "equal to" sign. When we use it between two numbers, it means that the numbers on both sides of the sign have the same value.

For example : 51 = 51

Greater Than >

This is the "greater than" sign. It is placed between two numbers in such a way that the open side is towards the bigger number.

For example : 46 > 32

Less Than <

This is the "less than" sign. It is placed between two numbers in such a way that the closed side is towards the smaller number.

For example : 52 < 67

Comparison of Numbers

Rule 1 : If a number has more digits than the other, then it is greater of the two. For example, 163 is greater than 35 i.e., 163 > 35.

Rule 2 : If two numbers have the same number of digits, the number with greater digit at the leftmost place is greater.

For example : 532 is greater than 432, i.e.,

```
532          432
 ↓            ↓
 5     >      4
```

Therefore, 532 > 432

Rule 3 : If the leftmost digits are also the same. We go to next digit from left and compare the next digits to the right, and so on.

For example, in 786 and 783,

$7 = 7$

And $8 = 8$

But, leftmost digit $6 > 3$.

Therefore, 786 > 783

Note: Count the digits first, then check H, then T, then O.

Successor of a Number

The number that comes just after a given number is called its **successor**.

Example : What is the successor of 99?

Solution : The successor of 99 = 99 + 1 = 100

Thus, we see that the successor of a number is obtained by adding 1 to that number.

Predecessor of a Number

The number that comes just before particular number is called its **predecessor**. So, we can find out the predecessor of a number by subtracting 1 from the number.

Example : What is the predecessor of 135?

Solution : The predecessor of 135 = 135 − 1 = 134

Even Numbers

The numbers that have 2, 4, 6, 8 and 0 in the ones place are called **even numbers**.

For example : 4, 8, 10, 32, 160, 496 are even numbers.

Odd Numbers

The numbers that have 1,3,5,7 and 9 in the ones place are called odd numbers.

For example : 3, 41, 49, 193 are **odd numbers**.

Properties of Odd and Even Numbers

(i) When we add an even number to an oddnumber the answer is always an odd number.

For example : 7 + 8 = 15

            odd even odd

(ii) When we add an odd number to an odd number, the answer is always an even number.

For example : 5 + 9 = 14

            odd odd even

(iii) When we add two even numbers the answer is always an even number.

For example : 6 + 4 = 10

            even even even

MUST REMEMBER

➡ A 3- digit number can be written in hundreds, tens and ones.

➡ Place value of a digit depends on its position in the given number. As the digit moves to the left, its value increases.

➡ Arranging the given numbers from smallest to the largest is called ascending order or increasing order.

➡ Arranging the given numbers from largest to the smallest is called descending order or decreasing order.

➡ The number that comes just after a given number is called its successor.

1. _____ is between 898 and 900.
   - (a) 897
   - (b) 901
   - (c) 898
   - (d) 899

2. What is the place value of 2 in 243?
   - (a) 200
   - (b) 2
   - (c) 20
   - (d) 0

3. 444 is _____ 4 + 4 + 4.
   - (a) Greater than
   - (b) less than
   - (c) Equal to
   - (d) None of these

4. 60 tens is _____ 7 hundreds.
   - (a) Greater than
   - (b) Less than
   - (c) Equal to
   - (d) None of these

5. Use the following clues to form a 3-digit number.
   - (i) The digit in the hundred place is 6 more than 2.
   - (ii) The digit in the tens place in an odd number is greater than 7.
   - (iii) The digit in the ones place is 2 less than the digit in the ends place.

   The number is _____.
   - (a) 698
   - (b) 672
   - (c) 896
   - (d) 272

6. The greatest 3-digit odd number is _____.
   - (a) 920
   - (b) 925
   - (c) 952
   - (d) 902

7. Which of the following number names does not show the number in the box?

   | 567 | 221 | 327 | 999 |

   - (a) Two hundred twenty-one
   - (b) Three hundred twenty-seven
   - (c) Five hundred sixty-seven
   - (d) Three hundred thirty-three

8. Which number is shown on the abacus?

   - (a) 643
   - (b) 246
   - (c) 245
   - (d) 346

9. The smallest 3-digit even number is __.
   - (a) 052
   - (b) 520
   - (c) 950
   - (d) 250

10. Which of the following number has 3 in tens place ?
    - (a) 323
    - (b) 396
    - (c) 438
    - (d) 943

11. The number having '3' in the hundreds place, '5' in the ones place and '2' in the tens place is _____:
    - (a) 352
    - (b) 532
    - (c) 253
    - (d) 325

12. Which symbol should be written in the box below to make the number sentence correct?

    432 ☐ 318
    - (a) >
    - (b) <
    - (c) =
    - (d) All of these

13. What number is 10 less than 205?
    - (a) 215
    - (b) 195
    - (c) 135
    - (d) 185

14. Which of the following statements is correct?
    (a) $321 < 235$
    (b) $420 > 510$
    (c) $725 < 638$
    (d) $827 > 639$

15. The smallest 3-digit number is_____ :
    (a) 999   (b) 100
    (c) 1000   (d) 99

16. Find the missing number from the following :
    $$597 = 500 + ... \times 10 + 7$$
    (a) 597   (b) 97
    (c) 90   (d) 9

17. Write down the numbers from 1 to 25 one after the other. Which digit is on the 25th place?
    (a) 7   (b) 5
    (c) 3   (d) 1

18. The greatest even number formed by the digits 3, 2 and 1 using only once is_____.
    (a) 321   (b) 312
    (c) 213   (d) 132

19. Which of the following is the predecessor of 390?
    (a) 389   (b) 393
    (c) 392   (d) 390

20. Look at these numbers :
    1 3 5 7 9 2 4 6 0 8
    Which number is fifth from the right?
    (a) 9   (b) 5
    (c) 2   (d) 4

21. Rajesh lost one of his chickens. Use the clues below to help him.

    Clue 1 : The digit in the ones place is 5.

    Clue 2 : The digit in the tens place is greater than the digit in the ones place.

    Clue 3 : The digit in the tens place is 7 more than the digit in the hundred place.

    Mark the correct chicken.

    (a) 185

    (b) 26

    (c) 115

    (d) 375

22. A boy has drawn a ball from a bag containing balls numbered from 1 to 100. It is found to be 19 more than the least two digit number. What is the number?

    (a) 10   (b) 19
    (c) 29   (d) 99

23. Golu wrote a number on the black board i.e.,

If it is formed from three different digits, then which number could be placed in the gap to make it the biggest number?

(a) 0   (b) 5

(c) 9   (d) 8

24. Golu has 387 stamps in his collection. What is 387 rounded to the nearest 10?

(a) 370   (b) 380

(c) 390   (d) 400

25. Ravi obtained 405, 365, 465, 307 and 495 marks in Class I, Class II, Class III, Class IV and Class V, respectively. He wants to arrange his marks in ascending order. What is the correct ascending order?

(a) 307, 405, 365, 465, 495

(b) 307, 365, 465, 405 , 495

(c) 307, 365, 405, 465, 495

(d) 365, 307, 405, 495, 465

HOTS

1. Which of the following statement is incorrect?

(a) There are 5 tens in 657.

(b) The place value of 7 in 976 is 70.

(c) 59 > 95

(d) 80 tens is equal to 8 hundreds.

2. The number shown on the abacus is____.

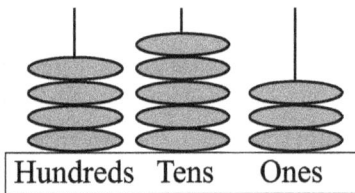

(a) 12   (b) 400

(c) 450   (d) 453

3. What is the expanded form of 956?

(a) 9 Hundreds + 6 tens + 5 ones

(b) 8 Hundreds + 9 tens + 8 ones

(c) 9 Hundreds + 8 tens + 8 ones

(d) 9 Hundreds + 5 tens + 6 ones

4. Fill the box.

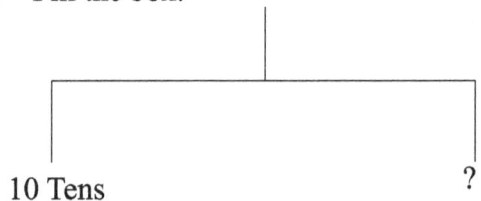

10 Tens

(a) 1 Hundred

(b) 90 Ones

(c) 2 Hundreds

(d) 10 Ones

5. Read the clues and find the number.
Clue 1: The digit at hundreds place is 2 more than the digit at ones place.
Clue 2 : The place value of 5 is 50.

(a) 735   (b) 975

(c) 957   (d) 846

1. What is successor of a numeral?

   Answer:

   The successor of a particular numeral comes just after that numeral. So, we can find out the successor of a numeral by adding 1 to the given numeral.

   e.g., The successor of 100 is 100 + 1 =101.

2. What is predecessor of a numeral?

   Answer:

   The predecessor of a particular numeral comes just before that numeral. So, we can find out the predecessor of a numeral by subtracting 1 from the given numeral.

   e.g., The predecessor of 100 is 100 - 1 = 99.

3. Ascending Order of numbers:

   Answer:

   Arranging numbers from the least number to the largest number is called Ascending Order. e.g., 13, 67,120,185 are numbers in ascending order.

4. Descending Order of numbers:

   Answer:

   Arranging numbers from the largest number to the least number is called Descending Order. e.g., 184, 120, 74, 13 are numbers in descending order.

5. What is the use of Symbol = ,< and >.

   Answer:

Symbol	Meaning	Example
= (is equal to)	The numbers on both the sides of = symbol have the same value.	25 = 25
< (is lesser than)	The number on the closed side of < symbol is lesser than the number on its open side.	23 < 28
> (is greater than)	The number on the open side of > symbol is greater than the number on its closed side.	35 > 25

Addition and Subtraction

Learning Objectives : In this chapter, students will learn about:
- ✓ Properties of Addition
- ✓ Properties of Subtraction

CHAPTER SUMMARY

Addition

Putting things together is called addition. It is denoted by the sign (+) called **plus**. To add 3-digit numbers, first we add ones, then tens and then hundreds.

Properties of Addition

(i)   While adding, if we change the order of the given numbers, the result will remain be the same.

(ii) The sum of three numbers is the same even if we change the grouping of the numbers.

(iii) When 0 is added to a number or a number is added to zero, the sum is the number itself.

For example : $198 + 0 = 198$
$$0 + 198 = 198$$

(iv) Addition of the 3-digit numbers is done by arranging the digits of ones, tens and hundreds in their proper place.

Addition of 3-digit numbers without carrying

Example : Add 376 and 213.

Solution :

Step 1 : Arrange the numbers according to their proper place values.

```
  H  T  O
  3  7  6
+ 2  1  3
---------
```

Step 2 : Add the ONES first, then the TENS and finally the HUNDREDS.

```
  H  T  O
  3  7  6
+ 2  1  3
---------
  5  8  9
```

Addition of 3-digit numbers with carrying

Example : Add 498 and 376.

Solution :

Step 1 : Arrange the digits of the numerals in proper places.

```
  H  T  O
  4  9  8
+ 3  7  6
---------
```

Step 2 : Add ones.
$$8 + 6 = 14$$
$$14 \text{ ones} = 1 \text{ ten} + 4 \text{ ones}$$

1 ten is carried to tens column and 4 is written in ones place.

Step 3 : Add tens.

$$1 + 9 + 7 = 17$$

17 tens = 1 hundred + 7 tens

1 hundred is carried to hundreds column and 7 is written in tens place.

Step 4 : Add hundreds. $1 + 4 + 3 = 8$

8 is written in hundreds place.

	1	**1**	
	4	9	8
+	3	7	6
	8	7	4

Therefore, $498 + 376 = 874$

Subtraction

Removing objects from a collection is called subtraction. It denoted by th sign (–) called **minus**.

Properties of subtraction

(i)   Zero subtracted from any number is equal to the number itself.

(ii) First we subtract ones then tens and then hundreds.

Subtraction of 3-digit number without borrowing

Example : Subtract 652 from 956.

Solution:

Step 1 : Arrange the numbers according to their proper place values.

	H	**T**	**O**
	9	5	6
–	6	5	2

Step 2 : Subtract ONES first, then the TENS and finally the HUNDREDS.

	H	**T**	**O**
	9	5	6
–	6	5	2
	3	0	4

Subtraction of 3-digit numbers with borrowing

Example : Subtract 652 from 831.

Solution:

Step 1 : Arrange the numbers according to their proper place values.

	H	**T**	**O**
	8	3	1
–	6	5	2

Step 2 : Subtract ones. $1 - 2 = ?$

We can't subtract 2 from 1. So we borrow 1 ten from 3 tens.

3 tens become 2 tens. 1 one become $10 + 1 = 11$ ones.

Subtract, $11 - 2 = 9$. Write 9 in ones place.

Step 3 : Subtract tens.

$2 - 5 = ?$

We can't subtract 5 from 2. So we borrow 1 hundred from 8 hundreds.

8 hundreds become 7 hundreds. 2 tens become $10 + 2 = 12$ tens.

Subtract, $12 - 5 = 7$. Write 7 in tens place.

Step 4 : Subtract hundreds. $7 - 6 = 1$

So we write 1 in place of hundreds.

	8	3	1
–	6	5	2
	1	7	9

Thus, we get $831 - 652 = 179$.

Note

To check the answer, we add the smaller of the two given numbers to the answer and if the sum thus obtained is equal to the larger given number, we say the answer is correct.

➡ Putting things together is called addition. It is denoted by the sign (+) called plus.

➡ When 0 is added to a number or a number is added to zero, the sum is the number itself.

➡ Removing objects from a collection is called subtraction. It denoted by th sign (–) called minus.

➡ Zero subtracted from any number is equal to the number itself.

1. 2 tens _____ ones + 4 tens 6 ones = 71
   (a) 5   (b) 15
   (c) 33   (d) 107

2. I am a 2- digit number. The sum of my 2 digits is 9. Their difference is 1. The bigger digit is in the tens place. What number am I?
   (a) 63   (b) 54
   (c) 81   (d) 76

3. Which of the following gives the greatest odd number as the answer?
   (a) 63 –18   (b) 80 – 14
   (c) 30 + 40   (d) 40 + 25

4. 14 is _____ more than 10 but _____ less than 24.
   (a) 4, 4   (b) 4, 10
   (c) 4, 14   (d) 34, 28

5. "I am more than 2+ 4 but less than 10 – 2. What number am I"?
   (a) 6   (b) 7
   (c) 8   (d) 2

6. 26 + 2 = _____ – 3
   (a) 24   (b) 25
   (c) 28   (d) 31

7. What must be added to 999 to get 1000?
   (a) 1   (b) 101
   (c) 9001   (d) 9999

8. 570 + 430 is equal to how many tens?
   (a) 100   (b) 43
   (c) 57   (d) 1000

9. Which number should be written in the box below to make the number sentence correct?

   $20 > \square + 10$
   (a) 5   (b) 10
   (c) 15   (d) 20

10. Which digit should come in place of '*'?

$$\begin{array}{r} 5 \\ + \ 3 \\ \hline 9 \end{array} \qquad \begin{array}{r} * \\ 8 \\ \hline 2 \end{array}$$

   (a) 4   (b) 3
   (c) 2   (d) 1

11. If we add 9 tens, 5 hundreds and 3 ones then the result is:
   (a) 395   (b) 17
   (c) 953   (d) 593

12. If the smallest 1-digit number is added to a number, we get:
   (a) It's predecessor
   (b) 2-digit number
   (c) It's successor
   (d) Can't say

13. Add me to 6 or subtract me from 14. The answer is the same. Who am I?
   (a) 14   (b) 10
   (c) 6   (d) 4

14. 786 – _____ = 5 less than 116.
   (a) 675   (b) 781
   (c) 670   (d) 791

15. The number with more digits is _____.
   (a) Always greater.
   (b) Sometimes greater.
   (c) Always smaller.
   (d) Can't say.

16. Difference between 25 and 205 is
_____.
    (a) 180　　　　　(b) 130
    (c) 30　　　　　(d) 230

17. 6 tens – 4 is equal to _____.
    (a) 64　　　　　(b) 56
    (c) 604　　　　(d) 640

18. What number replace question mark to make the number sentence true?
    $40 - ? = 24$
    (a) 38　　　　　(b) 64
    (c) 24　　　　　(d) 16

19. $\Delta + \square = 10$

    $\square - \Delta = 2$

    The two sentences shown above are true. Which of the following values for Δ and $\square$ make both number sentences true?
    (a) 4, 6　　　　(b) 8, 2
    (c) 7, 3　　　　(d) 8, 6

20. The sum of the numbers shown by two abacuses is _____.

    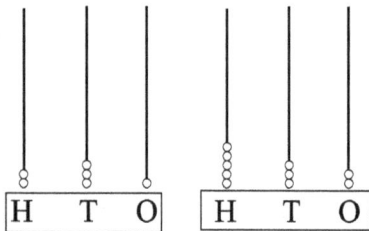

    (a) 750　　　　(b) 663
    (c) 763　　　　(d) 762

21. After spending ₹ 260, Hari had left ₹ 300. left. How did he have at first?

    (a) ₹ 300　　　　(b) ₹ 560
    (c) ₹ 40　　　　(d) ₹ 260

22. Rita collected 630 stamps. She gave 50 stamps to Ram. How many stamps had Rita left?
    (a) 580　　　　(b) 680
    (c) 620　　　　(d) 130

23. Bunny puts 235 jelly beans in a bottle. He needs 80 more jelly beans to fill up the bottle. How many jelly beans can the bottle hold?
    (a) 195　　　　(b) 395
    (c) 155　　　　(d) 315

24. Amit bought 2 items from his school bookshop. The items cost ₹ 50 in all. Which 2 items did he buy?.

Toy car	₹ 35
Story book	₹ 25
Pencil box	₹ 15
Water bottle	₹ 20

    (a) A pencil box and story book
    (b) A toy car and a story book
    (c) 2 water bottles
    (d) 2 story books

25. There are 300 students in a school. If 125 of them are girls, then find the number of boys.
    (a) 275　　　　(b) 175
    (c) 225　　　　(d) 169

HOTS

1. Find the values of x, y and z.

$$70 + x = 90$$
$$+$$
$$8$$
$$=$$
$$Y + 12 = Z$$

(a) 20, 98, 110   (b) 30, 100, 120
(c) 15, 95, 115   (d) 10, 90, 110

2. Shradha had ₹ 300. Her father gave her ₹ 550 as pocket money. She got ₹ 1000 from a price distribution in her school. How much money Shradha has now?
(a) ₹ 1300   (b) ₹ 850
(c) ₹ 1850   (d) ₹ 1550

3. Find P.

```
  8 P
- 5 4
  2 9
```
(a) 4   (b) 3
(c) 8   (d) 2

4. What must be subtracted from 956 to get 500?
(a) 200   (b) 256
(c) 456   (d) 500

5. Subtract the sum of 55 and 45 from the sum of 60 and 70.
(a) 20   (b) 15
(c) 5   (d) 30

SUBJECTIVE QUESTIONS

1. Tania has 17 pencils. Siya has 25 pencils. How many pencils are there in all?

```
Tanisha     1  7
Siya    +   2  5
```

Answer:

```
Tanisha     1  7
Siya    +   2  5
            4  2
```

There are 42 pencils in all.

2. In Muni's class, there are 13 English storybooks and 22 Hindi storybooks. How many storybooks are there in all?

```
      1  3
  +   2  2
```

Answer:

```
      1  3
  +   2  2
      3  5
```

There are 35 storybooks in all.

3. Shikha had 23 fruits. She ate 15 fruits. How many fruits are left?

$$\begin{array}{cc} & 2 \quad 3 \\ - & 1 \quad 5 \end{array}$$

Answer:

$$\begin{array}{cc} & 2 \quad 3 \\ - & 1 \quad 5 \\ \hline & 0 \quad 8 \end{array}$$

8 fruits are left.

4. Shekhar has 32 rupees. He bought a ball for 17 rupees. How much money is left with him?

$$\begin{array}{cc} & 3 \quad 2 \\ - & 1 \quad 7 \end{array}$$

Answer:

$$\begin{array}{cc} & 3 \quad 2 \\ - & 1 \quad 7 \\ \hline & 1 \quad 5 \end{array}$$

15 rupees are left with Shekhar.

5. Sheela bought biscuits for 24 rupees and a packet of chips for 16 rupees. How much money will she pay?

$$\begin{array}{cc} & 2 \quad 4 \\ + & 1 \quad 6 \end{array}$$

Answer:

$$\begin{array}{cc} & 2 \quad 4 \\ + & 1 \quad 6 \\ \hline & 4 \quad 0 \end{array}$$

Sheela pays 40 rupees.

Multiplication

3

> **Learning Objectives :** In this chapter, students will learn about:
> - ✓ Properties of Multiplication
> - ✓ Multiplying by Tens and Hundreds

CHAPTER SUMMARY

Multiplication

Multiplication is a repeated addition. The sign '×' is used for multiplication.

$6 + 6 + 6 = 18$ is the same as 6×3 (3 times 6).

We read 6 multiplied by 3 is 18.

Important Terms

(i)   The number to be multiplied is called the **Multiplicand**.

(ii) The number by which we multiply is called the **Multiplier**.

(iii) The result of multiplication is called the **Product**.

For example : $5 \times 3 = 15$

Here, 5 = Multiplicand, 3 = Multiplier, 15 = Product

Properties of Multiplication

(i)   The product of a number and zero is zero.

For example, $2 \times 0 = 0$

(ii) The product of a number and 1 is the number itself.

For example, $5 \times 1 = 5$

(iii) When the order of numbers is changed the product remains the same.

For example, $2 \times 3 = 3 \times 2 = 6$

Multiplication of 2-digit numbers by 1-digit number

Example : Multiply 98 by 3.

Step 1 : Multiply 8 ones by 3.

8 ones × 3 = 24 ones = 2 tens + 4 ones

Write 4 in the ones place and carry 2 tens to the tens place.

```
            2
        T   O
        9   8
      × 	  3
      ─────────
            4
```

Step 2 : Multiply 9 tens by 3.

9 tens × 3 = 27 tens

= 20 tens + 7 tens

= 2 hundreds + 7 tens

Write 2 in hundred place.

Add the carried 2 tens to 7 tens, we get 9 tens.

Write 9 in the tens place.

```
          2
      H   T   O
          9   8
      ×       3
      ───────────
      2   9   4
```

Multiplication of a 3- digit number by a 1-digit number

Multiply 154 by 3.

Step 1 : Multiply the ones.

4 ones 3=12 ones

12 ones = 1ten + 2 ones

Write 2 in the ones column and 1 as carry in tens column.

```
    H  T  O
          1
    1  5  4
    ×     3
          2
```

Step 2 : Multiply the tens.

5 tens × 3 = 15 tens

15 tens + 1 ten (carry) = 16 tens

16 tens = 1 hundred + 6 tens

Write 6 to the tens column and carry 1 the hundred column.

```
    H  T  O
    1  1
    1  5  4
    ×     3
       6  2
```

Step 3 : Multiply the hundreds.

1 hundred × 3 = 3 hundreds

3 hundreds + 1 hundred (carry) = 4 hundreds

Write 4 in the hundred column.

```
    H  T  O
    1  1
    1  5  4
    ×     3
    4  6  2
```

Multiplying by Tens and Hundreds

To multiply a given number by 10 and 100. We put one or two zeros, respectively to the right of the given number and get the product.

For example, $5 \times 10 = 50$

$6 \times 100 = 600$

Multiplying by 20, 30, 40, ..., 90

To multiply a given number by 20, 30, 40, ..., 90, we multiply the number by 2, 3, 4, ..., 9 and then we put one zero to the right of the product and get the answer.

For example:

$5 \times 10 = 5 \times 1$ tens = 5 tens = 50

$6 \times 30 = 6 \times 3$ tens = 18 tens = 180

$15 \times 60 = 15 \times 6$ tens = 90 tens = 900

TRIVIA

A circle possesses the largest area.

MUST REMEMBER

➡ Multiplication is a repeated addition.

➡ The product of a number and zero is zero.

➡ The product of a number and 1 is the number itself.

1. $6 + 6 + 6 + 6 + 6 + 6 + 6$

   = _____ $\times 6$ = _____
   (a) 5, 30   (b) 7, 42
   (c) 6, 36   (d) 6, 42

2. _____ $\times 8 = 96$
   (a) 12   (b) 88
   (c) 104   (d) 9

3. $4 \times 5 = 10 \times$ _____.
   (a) 0   (b) 1
   (c) 2   (d) 4

4. $7 + 7 + 7 + 7 + 7 + 7 =$ _____ $\times 7$
   (a) 1   (b) 5
   (c) 6   (d) 7

5. $17 \times 5 = (10 \times 5) + ($ _____ $\times 5)$
   (a) 1   (b) 3
   (c) 5   (d) 7

6. Find the value of A.
$$\begin{array}{r} A\,3 \\ \times\ 5 \\ \hline 2\,1\,5 \\ \hline \end{array}$$
   (a) 1   (b) 2
   (c) 3   (d) 4

7. Find the missing number.
   16, 20, 24, 28, ? 36, 40
   (a) 30   (b) 32
   (c) 34   (d) 38

8. 3×4 is _____ more than 2×4.
   (a) 2   (b) 3
   (c) 6   (d) 4

9. 9×5 is _____ more than 8×5.
   (a) 9   (b) 8
   (c) 5   (d) 1

10. $2 \times 10 = 4 \times$ _____
    (a) 5   (b) 8
    (c) 10   (d) 4

11. _____ $\times 10 = 5 \times 6$
    (a) 30   (b) 3
    (c) 5   (d) 60

12. There are 2 buttons in each t-shirt. How many buttons are there in 6 t-shirts?

    (a) 2   (b) 6
    (c) 24   (d) 12

13. There are 4 flowers in each pot. How many flowers are there in 5 pots?

    (a) 4   (b) 5
    (c) 20   (d) 10

14. Each chair has 4 legs. How many legs do 5 chairs have?

    (a) 4   (b) 5
    (c) 10   (d) 20

15. An ant has 6 legs. How many pairs of legs do 7 ants have?

1 pair of legs = 2 legs
(a) 21   (b) 42
(c) 7   (d) None of these

16. The product of 5 and 93 is _____.
(a) 455   (b) 456
(c) 465   (d) 451

17. 57×4 is the same as _____.
(a) 50 +7 +4   (b) 200 + 280
(c) 5×74 (d) 4×57

18. A T-shirt costs ₹29. What is the cost of 5 such T-shirts?
(a) ₹34   (b) ₹43
(c) ₹140   (d) ₹145

19. $32 \times 5 =$ _____ tens
(a) 6   (b) 16
(c) 60   (D) 160

20. $36 \times 0 =$ _____

(a) 36   (b) 1

(c) 0   (d) None of these

21. Raju bought the pencils. Each pencil cost ₹2. How much did the pencil cost altogether?

(a) ₹ 15   (b) ₹ 30
(c) ₹ 45   (d) ₹ 60

22. An art teacher bought 8 boxes of crayons. There were 10 crayons in each box. She bought _____ crayons. altogether.

(a) 10   (b) 20
(c) 40   (d) 80

23. Mrs. Raj sewed 4 skirts for her daughters. She sew 2 red buttons on each skirts. She sew 2 more pink buttons than red buttons. How many buttons did she sew altogether?
(a) 8   (b) 24
(c) 16   (d) 32

24. Shruti bought 8 packets of sweets. Each packet contained 5 sweets. She gave her brother 2 packets of sweets and ate 3 sweets. How many sweets did she have left?
(a) 30   (b) 34
(c) 35   (d) 27

25. Mother ordered 3 trays of eggs. Each tray contained 10 eggs. 4 eggs were rotten and 13 were cracked. How many good eggs were there?

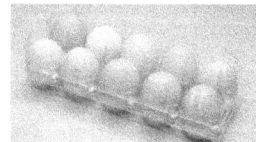

(a) 17   (b) 23
(c) 13   (d) 26

1. The number of legs of 8 rabbits is _____.
   (a) 16 tens + 5 ones
   (b) 32 ones
   (c) 3 tens − 2 tens
   (d) 2 tens − 4 ones

2. Apples are sold at ₹100 per kg. Jasmine has ₹1000. If she bought 5 kg of apples, how much money is left with her now?
   (a) 500   (b) 400
   (c) 600   (d) 100

3. Find P and Q.

   $$\begin{array}{r} 5\ P\ 3 \\ \times\ \ 4 \\ \hline Q\ 1\ 5 \\ \hline \end{array}$$

   (a) 2, 20   (b) 3, 27
   (c) 4, 26   (d) 2, 11

4. 4 + 4 + 4 + 4 + _____ = 32
   (a) 4 + 4 + 4
   (b) 4 + 4 + 4 + 4
   (c) 4 + 4 + 4 + 4 + 4
   (d) 4 + 4

5.

   $1 \times 6 = 6$

   $2 \times 6 = 12$

   $3 \times 6 = 18$

   ___ × ___ = ___

   (a) 3, 8, 24   (b) 4, 6, 24
   (c) 5, 5, 25   (d) 8, 8, 64

1. Multiply 36 by 25.

   Answer:

   Step - 1: First multiply ones.

	T	O
$6 \times 5 =$	3	0

   Write 0 in the ones place and carry 3 tens to the tens place.

   Step - 2: Multiply the digit in **tens** place of the multiplicand by the **ones** digit of the multiplier.

   $3 \times 5 = 15$.

   Now add the 3 carried from the product of ones to 15, which gives $15 + 3 = 18$. Write 18 beside 0 in the product.

   Step - 3: Now place a 0 below 0 in the product 180.

   $$\begin{array}{r} \ \ \ T\ \ O \\ 3\ \ 6 \\ \times\ \ 2\ \ 5 \\ \hline 1\ \ 8\ \ 0 \\ \hline \end{array}$$

   Multiply the digit 6 in **ones** place of the multiplicand by the digit 2 in **tens** place of multiplier.

   $6 \times 2 = 12$

   Write 2 below 8 in the product and carry 1 ten to the tens place.

③

```
      T   O
      3   6
  ×   2   5
  ─────────
  1   8   0
      2   0
```

Step - 4: Multiply 3 in the **tens** place by 2 in the tens place of the multiplier.

$3 \times 2 = 6$. Add the 1 carried from previous product to get $6 + 1 = 7$.

Now, write 7 below 1 in 180.

```
      T   O
      3   6
  ×   2   5
  ─────────
      1   8   0
  +   7   2   0
  ─────────
      9   0   0
```

Now, add the products and write the sum which is the required product of the two given numbers.

Hence, $36 \times 25 = 900$

2. Fill in the blank with suitable number.

5, 10, 15, _____, 25, 30, ...

Answer:

This can be found with the help of table of 5. Hence, in the blank space, 20 is suitable number.

3. Which number should be multiplied with 9 to get the result 54?

Answer:

54 is at the sixth place in the table of 9. Therefore, 6 should be multiplied with 9 to get 54.

4. A factory produces 15 items in a day. How many items it will produce in a week if Sunday is a holiday?

Answer:

Items produced in a day = 15

Items produced in 6 days = $15 \times 6 = 90$ items.

5. The cost of potato is 10 rupees per kg. What is the cost of 3 Kg of potatoes?

Answer:

Required cost = Quantity of potato × Cost of potato = $3 \times 10 = 30$ rupees.

Division

4

CHAPTER SUMMARY

Division

Division is a process of dividing into groups. It is also considered as a process of repeated subtraction or a process of distribution equally among a group.

Sharing and subtracting repeatedly are two of the basic ways of dividing. We also use multiplication tables in dividing.

Basic Terms

- **Dividend :** The number that we divide is. called the dividend.
- **Divisor :** he number by which we dvide is called the divisor.
- **Quotient :** It is the result obtained on division.
- **Remainder :** If there is a number leftover, it is called the remainder.

Dividend = Divisor × Quotient + Remainder

For example :

$$\text{Divisor} \longrightarrow 6\,\overline{)\,34\,}\,(5$$

Dividend — 34, Quotient — 5, Remainder — 4

Properties of Division

(i). In division, the remainder has to be either '0' or less than divisor.

(ii). If we divide a number by the number itself, then the quotient is 1.

(iii) If we divide a number by 1, then the quotient is the same as the dividend.

(iv) We cannot divide any number by zero.

(v) When 0 is divided by any number (other than zero) the quotient is zero.

Equal-Sharing

Example : I have 12 apples with me and I want to distribute them equally among 3 boys. How many apples will each boy get?

Solution :

Step 1 : Give one apple to each boy.

boy-1   boy-2   boy-3

We have, 12 – 3 = 9 apples left.

Step 2 : Again give 1 apple to each boy from the remaining apples.

boy-1   boy-2

boy-3

We have, $9 - 3 = 6$ apples left.

Step 3 : Give 1 more apple to each boy.

boy-1   boy-2

boy-3

We have, $6 - 3 = 3$ apples left.

Step 4 : Again give 1 apple to each boy.

boy-1   boy-2

boy-3

We have, $3 - 3 = 0$. Each boy has got 4 apples and no apples left.

We observed that 12 apples have been distributed among 3 boys. Each boy got 4 apples.

Thus $12 \div 3 = 4$

Grouping

Example : 9 balls are to be distributed among some boys. Each boy should get 3 balls. How many boys are there?

Solution :

Step 1 : Give 3 balls to one boy.

We have, $9 - 3 = 6$ balls left.

Step 2 : Give 3 balls to the next boy.

We have, $6 - 3 = 3$ balls left.

Step 3 : Give 3 balls to the next boy.

We have, $3 - 3 = 0$

No balls left, we observed that, Three boys got the balls.

boy 1 →

boy 2 →

boy 3 →

Thus, $9 \div 3 = 3$

Multiplication and Division Facts

$$20 \div 4 = 5$$

Example: $5 \times 4 = 20$

$$20 \div 5 = 4$$

Long Division

Example : Divide 93 by 4 using long division.

Solution:

Step 1 : Arrange the numbers in the following manner.

$$4 \overline{)\,93\,(}$$

Step 2 : We divide from left. We see $4 \times 2 = 8$ less than 9 and $4 \times 3 = 12$ greater than 9. We take 2 as the quotient.

$$4 \times 2 = 8$$
$$9 - 8 = 1$$

$$
\begin{array}{r}
4\,\overline{)\,9\;3\,}\,(23 \\
-8 \\
\hline
1\,3 \\
-1\,2 \\
\hline
1
\end{array}
$$

Step 3 : We see $4 \times 3 = 12$ less than, $4 \times 4 = 16$ greater than 13.

We take 3 as the quotient

$$4 \times 3 = 12$$
$$13 - 12 = 1$$

So, 1 is the remainder.

Thus, $93 \div 4 = 23$, remainder $= 1$

Verification

Dividend = Divisor × Quotient + Remainder

$$93 = 4 \times 23 + 1$$
$$= 92 + 1$$
$$= 93$$

The answer is verified.

TRIVIA

The number 0.999999 is equal to 1.

Tests of Division

(i)   A number with 0, 2, 4, 6 or 8 at ones place is divisible by 2.

(ii) If the sum of the digits of a given number is divisible by 3, then the number is divisible by 3.

(iii) A number with" 0" or" 5"at ones place is divisible by 5.

(iv) A number with "0" at ones place is divisible by 10.

MUST REMEMBER

➡ Division is a process of dividing into groups. It is also considered as a process of repeated subtraction or a process of distribution equally among a group.

➡ If we divide a number by the number itself, then the quotient is 1.

➡ If we divide a number by 1, then the quotient is the same as the dividend.

➡ We cannot divide any number by zero.

1. $4 = 32 \div$ _____
   (a) 16   (b) 8
   (c) 4   (d) 2

2. $12 \div 4 = 9 \div$ _____
   (a) 9   (b) 4
   (c) 3   (d) 1

3. $42 \div 7 =$ _____
   (a) 5   (b) 6
   (c) 7   (d) 8

4. Which number is missing in the number sentence?
   $63 \div$ _____ $= 7$
   (a) 6   (b) 7
   (c) 8   (d) 9

5. In which number sentence does 4 make the equation true?
   (a) $40 \div$ _____ $= 8$
   (b) $24 \div$ _____ $= 8$
   (c) $32 \div$ _____ $= 8$
   (d) $16 \div$ _____ $= 8$

6. $(27 \div 3) \times 8 =$ _____
   (a) 24   (b) 27
   (c) 42   (d) 72

7. If we start subtracting 4 from 19 stepwise as shown, we will be able to subtract 4 times.
   $$19 - 4 = 15$$
   $$15 - 4 = 11$$
   $$11 - 4 = 7$$
   $$7 - 4 = 3$$
   If we start subtracting 4 from 84 in a similar manner, how many times will we be able to subtract?
   (a) 21   (b) 42
   (c) 68   (d) 84

8. If this pattern continues, then what is the next number?
   80, 40, 20, _____
   (a) 10   (b) 15
   (c) 30   (d) 5

9. 3 tens $\div 3 =$ _____
   (a) 1   (b) 10
   (c) 90   (d) 100

10. How many threes are there in the sum of 63 and 27.
    (a) 3   (b) 9
    (c) 21   (d) 30

11. _____ $\div 3 = 5 \times 5$
    (a) 15   (b) 75
    (c) 90   (d) 60

12. If $5 \times 3 = 15$ then $15 \div 3 =$ _____
    (a) 15   (b) 3
    (c) 5   (d) 4

13. If $6 \times 4 =$ _____ then _____ $\div 4$
    $=$ _____
    (a) 24, 24, 6   (b) 24, 6, 24
    (c) 24, 4, 24   (d) 24, ,24, 4

14. $20 \div 1 =$ _____
    (a) 1   (b) 20
    (c) 0   (d) 2

15. _____ $\div 7 = 0$
    (a) 1   (b) 0
    (c) 7   (d) 14

16. If $40 \div 4 = 10$, then quotient is _____

    (a) 0   (b) 40

    (c) 4   (d) 10

17. If $18 \div 3 =$ _____ then the dividend is _____.

    (a) 6, 18   (b) 5, 18   (c) 6, 3   (d) 5, 3

18. If $2 \times 6 = 12$ then _____ $\div 6 =$ _____ and _____ $\div 2 =$ _____.

    (a) 12, 12, 6 ,6   (b) 2, 12, 6, 12

    (c) 2, 12, 12, 6   (d) 12, 2, 12, 6

19. Make groups of two. How many groups do you get?

    (a) 10   (b) 5
    (c) 3   (d) 4

20. 3 Boys shared following balls equally among themselves. How many balls did each boy get?

    (a) 6   (b) 4

    (c) 3   (d) 2

21. A gardener has 70 potted plants. He arranges 10 potted plants in each row. There are _____ rows of potted plants.

    (a) 70   (b) 10
    (c) 700   (d) 7

22. Amita had 36 apples, among them 9 apples were rotten. She kept the rest in bags. How many bags did Amita use if each bag had 3 apples?

    (a) 27   (b) 12
    (c) 9   (d) 3

23. There are 5 baskets and 10 apples. The apples are shared equally among 5 baskets. How many apples does each basket have?

    (a) 10   (b) 8
    (c) 5   (d) 2

24. Mona arranges 15 tables into 3 equal rows. Each row have _____ tables.
    (a) 15   (b) 8
    (c) 3   (d) 5

25. Bunny took three days to finish reading a book of 36 pages. How many pages did he read a day?
    (a) 4   (b) 12
    (c) 13   (d) 33

1. How many bunches of 6 bananas can be formed from the given bunches of 12 bananas?

(a) 20   (b) 18

(c) 15   (d) 12

2. How many bunches of 5 cherries can be formed from given bunches of cherries?

(a) 4   (b) 5

(c) 3   (d) 2

3. Find the dividend if :
Divisor   = 16
Quotient   = 7
Remainder   = 2
(a) 110   (b) 112
(c) 114   (d) 120

4. $0 \div (2 \times 4 + 5 \times 5) = $ _____.
(a) 5   (b) 10
(c) 15   (d) 0

5. Divide the sum of 92 and 52 by the sum of 9 and 7?
(a) 9   (b) 8
(c) 10   (d) 12

1. How many bundles of 8 pencils can you make out of 400 pencils?

Answer:

Total number of pencil divided by one bundle of pencil = 400 ÷ 8 = 50 bundles.

2. If a minibus can carry 28 children then how many mini buses would be needed to carry 392 children?

Answer:

Total number of children is divided by capacity of one mini- bus (28 children) 392 ÷ 28 = 14 minibus.

3. Divide 93 by 4 using long division method

Step 1: Arrange the numbers in the following manner.

4)93(

Step 2: We divide from left.

$4 \times 2 = 8$

which is less than 9 and

$4 \times 3 = 12$

greater than 9

We take 2 as quotient

$4 \times 2 = 8$

$9 - 8 = 1$

Step 3: We see

$4 \times 3 = 12$

which is less than 13 and

$4 \times 4 = 16$

which is more than 13.

```
      23
4 ) 93 (
    -8
    ───
    13
    12
    ──
     1  ←── Remainder
    ───
```

4. A man spent Rs. 1050 on 5 T-shirts. What is the cost of each T-shirt?

    Answer:

    The price of 5T-Shirts is Rs. 1050 The price of 1 T-Shirt is Rs. 1050 ÷ 5

    ```
    3 ) 93 ( 31
        −9↓
        ───
         03
          3
        ───
          0
    ```

    Therefore price of one T-Shirt is Rs. 210.

5. Auli has 16 bananas. She wanted to share her bananas with her 7 friends. How many bananas will each one get including Auli?

    Answer:

    Auli has 16 bananas and she wanted to divide the bananas with her 7 friends including Auli that means 16 bananas should be divided in 8 persons. Therefore each person will get 2 bananas.

Measurement

5

CHAPTER SUMMARY

Length

We can measure lengths with the help of a tape or metre rod or a metre scale. The standard unit of length is metre.

1 metre = 100 centimetres

In short, centimetre is written as cm and metre is written as m.

1 kilometre = 1000 metres

For example, (i) The giraffe is 12 m tall.

12 m

(ii) The boy is 2 m tall.

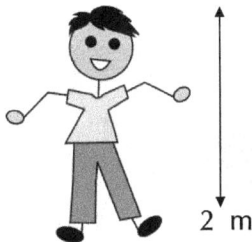

2 m

The giraffe (12 m) is taller than the boy (2 m). The total height of the giraffe and the boy
= 12 + 2 = 14 m

Weight

The weight of rice, sugar, vegetables and other articles are weighted in terms of kilo grams and grams. The standard unit of mass is **kilogram**. Kg is the short form of kilogram and '*g*' is the short form of gram.

Here are some common weights used with weighting scales :

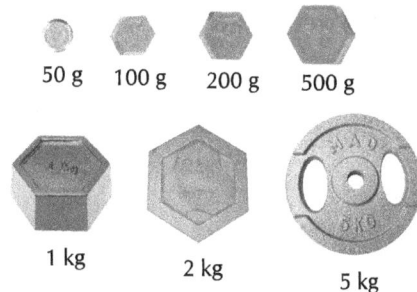

50 g   100 g   200 g   500 g

1 kg   2 kg   5 kg

Along with these, smaller weight like, 1 g, 2 g, 5 g, 10 g and 20 g are also used.

- 1 kg = 1000 g
- Half a kg $= \dfrac{1000}{2} = 500$ g

There are different types of scales. Each marking on the scale stands for different weight :

Each marking stands for 100 gm.

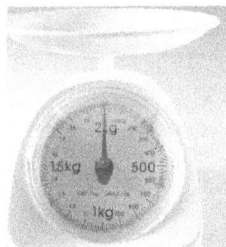

Each marking stands for 20 kg.

Capacity

The capacity of a container is the maximum quantity of the liquid like milk, oil, water, etc. which it can hold. The standard unit for measuring the capacity of a container is litre.

1 litre = 1000 millilitre

Liquids in small quantities are measured in millilitres.

Liquids are measured by special vessels.

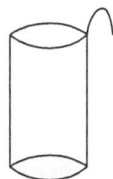 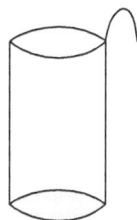

200 mL   500 mL   100 mL = 1L

In short, litre is written as 'L' and millilitre as ml. The smaller quantities of liquids like medicines are generally measured in terms of millilitres.

For example : This is a carton of juice. It contains 1L of orange juice.

This is a can of coke. It contains less than 1litre of coke.

TRIVIA

The result of $(6 \times 9) + (6 + 9)$ is 69.

MUST REMEMBER

➤ The weight of rice, sugar, vegetables and other articles are weighted in terms of kilo grams and grams.

➤ Liquids in small quantities are measured in millilitres.

MULTIPLE CHOICE QUESTIONS

Direction (1–5) : Study the picture and answer the following questions :

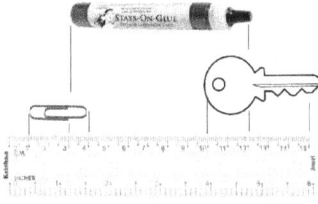

1. The paperclip is _____ cm long.
   - (a) 1
   - (b) 3
   - (c) 4
   - (d) 2

2. The glue is _____ cm long.
   - (a) 6
   - (b) 10
   - (c) 7
   - (d) 9

3. The key is _____ cm long.
   - (a) 2
   - (b) 7
   - (c) 5
   - (d) 4

4. The total length of the key, glue and paperclip is _____ cm.
   - (a) 12
   - (b) 17
   - (c) 15
   - (d) 10

5. _____ paperclips will add up to the length of 1 glue.
   - (a) 2
   - (b) 3
   - (c) 4
   - (d) 5

Direction (6–10) : Study the given figure and answer the following questions :

Flour	Coffee Powder	Biscuits
350 gm	150 gm	200 gm

6. The weight of the packet of biscuits is- _____ g lighter than the weight of the packet of flour.

   - (a) 300
   - (b) 200
   - (c) 150
   - (d) 250

7. The weight of 2 packets of flour is _____ g.
   - (a) 800
   - (b) 750
   - (c) 500
   - (d) 700

8. The weight of 4 packets of biscuits is _____ g.
   - (a) 800
   - (b) 300
   - (c) 650
   - (d) 700

9. The weight of 1 bag of flour is _____ g less than 4 packets of biscuits.
   - (a) 250
   - (b) 350
   - (c) 450
   - (d) 300

10. The total weight of 1 bag of flour, 1 packet of coffee powder and 1 packet of biscuit is _____ g.
    - (a) 400
    - (b) 300
    - (c) 700
    - (d) 500

Direction (11–15) : Water in each of the following containers is poured into cups. Study the picture and answer the following questions :

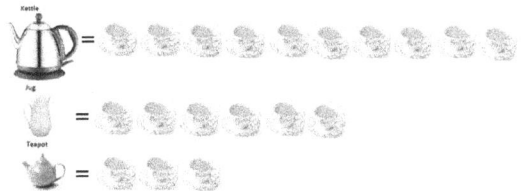

11. _____ cups of tea can fill 3 teapots.
    - (a) 6
    - (b) 8
    - (c) 9
    - (d) 7

12. The _____ has the least amount of tea.
    - (a) Kettle
    - (b) Teapot
    - (c) Jug
    - (d) Kettle and jug

13. The _____ has the most amount of tea.
   - (a) Jug
   - (b) Teapot
   - (c) Kettle
   - (d) Kettle and jug

14. The _____ holds 5 fewer cups of tea than the kettle.
   - (a) Jug
   - (b) Teapot
   - (c) Can't say
   - (d) None of these

15. The total volume of teapot and the jug is_____ more cup of the tea than the kettle.
   - (a) 2
   - (b) 3
   - (c) 4
   - (d) 1

16. What is the weight of the pineapple?

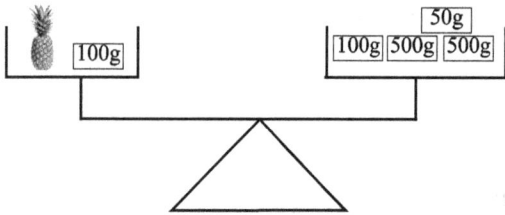

   - (a) 500g
   - (b) 1Kg
   - (c) 1 kg 50g
   - (d) 100g

17. What is the difference between heights of both the trees?

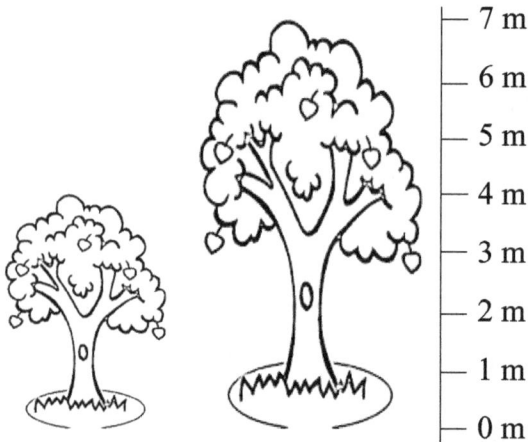

   - (a) 2 m
   - (b) 3 m
   - (c) 4 m
   - (d) 5 m

18. Which block is heaviest among all four?
   - (a) 150 Kg
   - (b) 1 Kg 50 g
   - (c) 1.50 Kg
   - (d) 15000g

19. If ⊔ + ⊔ + ⊔ = 3 Litres, then ⊔ = _____
   - (a) 2 Litres
   - (b) 1 Litre
   - (c) 3 Litres
   - (d) None of these

20. How much more weight should be put to balance the weighing machine?

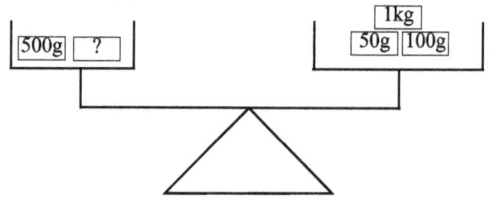

   - (a) 400 g
   - (b) 650 Kg
   - (c) 650 g
   - (d) 600 g

21. The distance between Veeru's home and his school is 456 m. After walking 187m. from his home, Veeru realized that he forgot it bring his pencil box. He walked back home to get it and then walked to school. What is the total distance travelled by him?
   - (a) 269 + 187
   - (d) 456 + 187
   - (c) 456 + 187 + 187
   - (d) 266 + 187

22. Seema is taking part in a race. She has to run for 500 m, swim for 350 m, and then cycle for another 150 m. After one hour, she still have 45 m more to complete. What distance travelled by Seema in one hour?
   - (a) 1045 m
   - (b) 955 m
   - (c) 1000 m
   - (d) 910 m

23. A snail fell into a well. The well is 30 m tall. Every day, it can climb 6 m but will sip 2 m down. How many days will take to reach the top?
    (a) 8
    (b) 7
    (c) 6
    (d) 5

24. A packet of milk is 432 g heavier than a packet of orange juice . The weight of the packet of orange juice is 212 g. What is the total mass of the packet of milk and orange juice?

    (a) 950
    (b) 856
    (c) 986
    (d) 748

25. Amit's weight is 50 kg. He is 4 kg heavier than Meena. Balaji is 5 kg heavier than Amit. Total weight of all is _____ kg.
    (a) 165
    (b) 160
    (c) 151
    (d) 132

HOTS

1. It takes 12 glasses of water to fill up the jug. It takes 3 bowls to fill a glass. How many bowls of water will be required to fill the jug?

    (a) 12
    (b) 36
    (c) 24
    (d) None of these

Directions 2 : Look at the diagram below and answer the given questions :

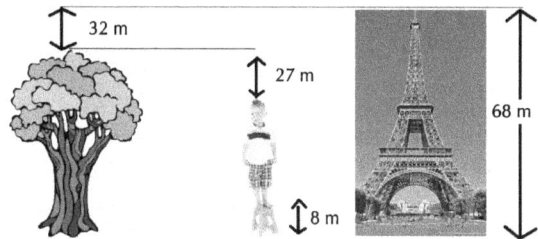

2. The tree is _____ m tall.
    (a) 36
    (b) 34
    (c) 28
    (d) 32

3. Sita weighs 40 kg. Kavita weighs 4 kg less than Sita. Rina weighs 6 kg more than Kavita. What is the weight of Kavita?
    (a) 30 kg
    (b) 36 kg
    (c) 42 kg
    (d) 40 kg

Direction (4–5)

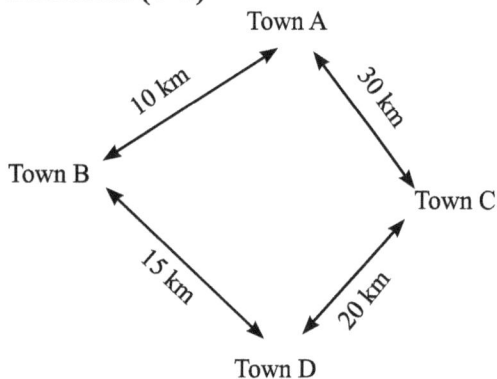

4. What is the total distance that Kavya needs to cover to go to town B from A by crossing town C and town D?
   (a) 30 km   (b) 10 km
   (c) 65 km   (d) 70 km

5. What is the shortest distance from town A to town B?
   (a) 30 km   (b) 10 km
   (c) 65 km   (d) 70 km

SUBJECTIVE QUESTIONS

1. John bought the following items from the market: 3 kg 500 grams of potatoes, 4 kg 200 grams of onions and 2 kg 700 grams of green vegetables. What is the total weight of the items?

   Answer:

   Total weight = 3 kg 500 grams + 4 kg 200 grams + 2 kg 700 grams = 9 kg 1400 grams = 10 kg 400 grams.

2. To obtain the volume of oil in litres how much quantity of oil is required in a container, which already contains 45 litres 900 millilitres of oil?

   Answer:

   45 litres 900 millilitres of oil becomes 46 litres when 100 millilitres is added to it.

3. What will be the length of each equal side of a triangle, if the sum of the length of its three sides is 15 cm?

   Answer:

   Each side = 15/3 = 5 cm.

4. A travels 56 km and B travels 39 km. Who travels the longer distance and by how much?

   Answer:

   Since 56 > 39 and 56−39=17

   Therefore, A travels longer distance by 17 km.

5. What will be the 10th part of a line segment of length 50 cm?

   Answer:

   10th part of 50 cm refers to 50 / 10. Hence, the 10th part of line segment will be 5 cm.

Time

6

CHAPTER SUMMARY

Time

See the clock given below. It has three hands, the shorter hand **(hour hand)**, the longer hand **(minute hand)** and the longest and thin **(second hand)**. The face of the clock is divided into 12 equal big division marked as 1, 2, 3, 4, …. There are five small division between two successive number. So, there are 60 small division in all.

The time shown in the clock is 5.30.

We read it as five thirty.

If it is in the morning, we write the time as 5.30 am.

If it is at night, we write the time as 5.30 pm.

We use am for time from 12 midnight to just before noon.

We use pm for time from 12 noon to just before midnight.

Important Points

(i) We write minutes as min and hour as "h".

(ii) There are 60 minutes in 1 hour.

(iii) There are 60 seconds in 1 minute.

(iv) In 60 minutes, the minute hand moves one complete round.

See the following example :

In 1 hour, the hour hand moves from 9 to 10.

> 7 am is 1 hour before 8 am.
> 8 am is 1 hour after 7 am.

Before and After

Mr. Ankit woke up at 7 am. He left for work at 8 am.

Mr. Ankit took 1 hour to get ready for work.

Mr. Ankit reached his office at 8.30 am.

Mr. Ankit took 30 minutes to travel to his office.

8 am is 30 minutes before 8:30 am.

8:30 am is 30 minutes after 8 am.

Some Conversions

(i) 1 hour = 60 minutes, 1 minute = 60 seconds

1 hour = 60 × 60 = 3600 seconds

(ii) 1 day = 24 hours, 1 week = 7 days, 1 month = 4 weeks, 1 year = 12 months,

1 year = 52 weeks, 1 year = 365 days

Calendar

Calendar is a diagram that shows what day and month it is.

Months

There are twelve months in a year:

Here are the twelve months in detail :

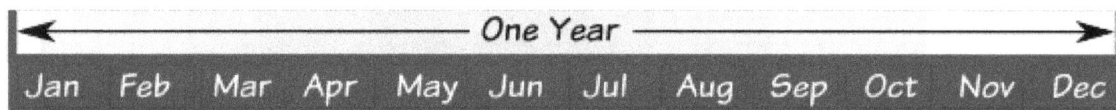

Month Number	Month	In 3 letters	Days in Month
1	January	Jan	31
2	February	Feb	28 (29 in leap years)
3	March	Mar	31
4	April	Apr	30
5	May	May	31
6	June	Jun	30
7	July	Jul	31
8	August	Aug	31
9	September	Sep	30
10	October	Oct	31
11	November	Nov	30
12	December	Dec	31

February

The shortest month of all is February. February has only 28 days, but on Leap years February has 29 days!

Knuckle Method

To remember number of days, you can use the "knuckle method" :

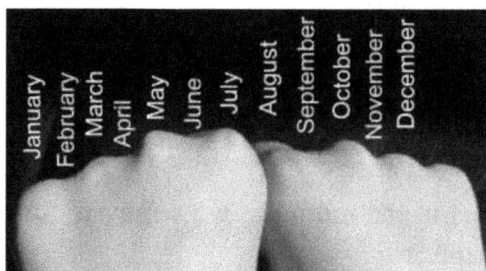

A knuckle is "31 days", and in between each knuckle it isn't. And where you hands meet, the two knuckles are "July, August", which both have 31 days.

(**Note :** the last knuckle isn't used.)

Example : March is on a knuckles, so it has 31 days

Seasons

The year is divided into five seasons:

(i)   Summer season (*Grishma*)

(ii) Rainy Season (*Varsha*)

(iii) Autumn Season (*Sharada*)

(iv) Pre-winter Season (*Hemanta*)

(v)   Winter season (*Shishira*)

TRIVIA

The two sentences, "twelve plus one" and "eleven plus two", both have 13 letters.

MUST REMEMBER

➡ There are 60 minutes in 1 hour.
➡ There are 60 seconds in 1 minute.
➡ In 60 minutes, the minute hand moves one complete round.

MULTIPLE CHOICE QUESTIONS

1. The minute hand takes _____ minutes to move from 3 to 9.
   (a) 6
   (b) 10
   (c) 20
   (d) 30

2. How many days are there in February 2008?
   (a) 28
   (b) 29
   (c) 30
   (d) 31

3. How many minutes are there in one day?
   (a) 1440
   (b) 86400
   (c) 76000
   (d) 2440

4. The table below shows the number of months in different number of years.

   Months in Years

Number of years	1	2	3
Number of months	12	24	36

   What is one way to find the number of months in 7 years?
   (a) Multiply 7 by 12
   (b) Add 12 to 7
   (c) Subtract 7 from 12
   (d) Divide 12 by 7

5. When the short hand is at 4 and the long hand is at 12, the time is :
   (a) 4 O'clock
   (b) 12 O'clock
   (c) 8 O'clock
   (d) 3 O'clock

6 How many months in a year have 31 days?
   (a) 8
   (b) 7
   (c) 6
   (d) 5

7. How many times does long hand of a clock take to complete its three rounds?
   (a) 2 hours
   (b) 2 hours 30 minutes
   (c) 60 minutes
   (d) 3 hours

8. The month with neither 31 days nor 30 days is _____
   (a) February
   (b) April
   (c) November
   (d) December

9. 135 hours = _____
   (a) 5 days
   (b) 5 days 10 hours
   (c) 5 days 15 hours
   (d) None of these

10. How many months in a year have 30 days?
   (a) 6
   (b) 5
   (c) 4
   (d) None of these

11. The hour hand takes _____ hours to move from 2 to 5.
   (a) 3
   (b) 1
   (c) 2
   (d) 6

12. 105 hours = _____
   (a) 4 days
   (b) 4 days 9 hours
   (c) 4 days 15 hours
   (d) None of these

13. The month with 31 days is _____.
   (a) February
   (b) April
   (c) November
   (d) December

14. The month with 30 days is/are _____.
   (a) April
   (b) November
   (c) June
   (d) All of these

15. When the short hand is at 2 and the long hand is at 12, the time is _____ .
    (a) 2 O'clock   (b) 12 O'clock
    (c) 14 O'clock   (d) None of these

16. Rohan starts his football practice from Monday. If he practices only for one week, then what is the last day of his practice? (Include Sunday also)
    (a) Tuesday   (b) Monday
    (c) Sunday   (d) Wednesday

17. Which clock shows half past three?

    (i)   (ii)   (iii)   (iv)
    (a) (i)   (b) (ii)
    (c) (iii)   (d) (iv)

18. A clock is 25 mins slow. What is the actual time, if it is showing 5:00 p.m.?
    (a) 4:35 pm   (b) 5:30 pm
    (c) 5:25 pm   (d) 5: 25 am

19. What is the time, if it is 15 mins before 5:40 am?
    (a) 5:25am   (b) 5:30am
    (c) 5:45am   (d) 5:35am

20. Match the following :
    (A) Summer   1. Rainy
    (B) Hemanta   2. Hot
    (C) Varsha   3. Cold
    (D) Spring   4. Vasanta

	A	B	C	D
(a)	2	3	1	4
(b)	1	2	3	4
(c)	2	1	3	4
(d)	3	4	1	2

21. Mecna's ballet class is at 10 am. Her lesson ends 45 minutes later. What time did her lesson end ?
    (a) 9:15 am   (b) 10:45 am
    (c) 9:30 am   (d) 9:45 am

22. Heena takes 5 minutes to draw a cookie. How long does she takes to draw 9 similar cookies?
    (a) 40 min   (b) 35 min
    (c) 45 min   (d) 50 min

23. Nanu was born on 29 of February. Her birthday comes _____ .
    (a) Every year
    (b) Twice in a year
    (c) After every four years
    (d) After every two years

24. Golu's violin lesson started at 9 am. The lesson lasted for 1 hour. The lesson ended at _____ .
    (a) 8:00 am   (b) 10:00 am
    (c) 8:00 pm   (d) 10:00 pm

25. Bhola watch a cartoon programme which lasted 30 minutes. The programme ended at 2.30 pm. The programme started at _____ .
    (a) 2:30 pm   (b) 3:00 pm
    (c) 2:00 am   (d) 2:00 pm

Time

1. Sheetal started walking to temple at 5:25 p.m. She reached the temple at 5.50 p.m. How long did she take to walk to the temple?
   - (a) 20 mins
   - (b) 25 mins
   - (c) 30 mins
   - (d) 35 mins

2. Ankit starts his guitar parctice from 1st November 20XX. He practices for 10 days and then takes 2 days break. Again he practices for 2 days, his practice finishes on _____.

   November 20XX

Mon	Tue	Wed	Thu	Fri	Sat	Sun
				1	2	3
4	5	6	7	8	9	10
11	12	13	14	15	16	17
18	19	20	21	22	23	24
25	26	27	28	29	30	

   - (a) 13th November
   - (b) 15th November
   - (c) 14th November
   - (d) 16th November

3. If I take 45 mins to take one round of a park, then how much time I will take to complete three rounds of the same park?
   - (a) 1 Hour
   - (b) 2 Hours 15 Minutes
   - (c) 2 Hours
   - (d) 1 Hours 20 Minutes

4. Aman, Raman and Kamal leave school at 2 p.m. for their respective homes. Aman reaches his house at 2:30 p.m., Raman reaches his house at 2:45 p.m. and Kamal reaches his house at 3:10 p.m. Who took least time to reach?
   - (a) Aman
   - (b) Raman
   - (c) Kamal
   - (d) Aman and Raman

5. Aman takes 45 minutes to solve a Maths paper and 50 minutes to solve an English paper How much time will he take to solve both papers?
   - (a) 1 hours 40 minutes
   - (b) 2 hours
   - (c) 3 hours
   - (d) 1 hours 35 minutes

SUBJECTIVE QUESTIONS

1. 10 minutes means___ times of _____ seconds.

   Answer:

   1 minute = 60 seconds

   Hence, 10 minutes = 600 seconds i.e 10 times of 60 seconds.

2. Convert 5 hours in seconds.

   Answer:

   1hour = 60 × 60 = 3600 seconds.

   So, 5 hour = 5 × 3600 seconds = 18000 Seconds

3. Two trains leave from Hyderabad and arrive at Secunderabad at the times shown in the time-table given.

Train Time Table		
Train	Leaves from Hyderabad	Arrives at Secunderabad
Express	5 : 10 p.m.	5 : 40 p.m.
Local	5 : 30 p.m.	6 : 20 p.m.

What is the difference in the times taken by the local train and the express train to go from Hyderabad to Secunderabad?

Answer:

Time taken by the express train to go from Hyderabad to Secunderabad = (5:40 – 5:10) p.m. = 30 minutes

Time taken by the local train = (6:20 – 5:30) p.m. = 50 minutes.

So, the required difference = 50 – 30 = 20 minutes.

4. Golu watched a cartoon programme for 30 minutes. If the programme ended at 2:30 p.m., when did it start?

Answer:

30 minutes before 2:30 p.m. is 2:00 p.m.

5. How many minutes after 7: 30 is 8: 30?

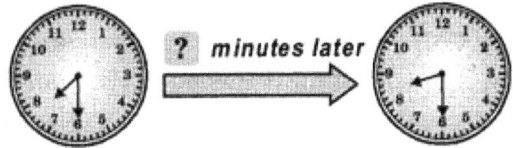

Answer:

The time between 7:30 and 8:30 is 1 hour which is 60 minutes.

Money

Learning Objectives : In this chapter, students will learn about:
- ✓ Money
- ✓ Important Points about Money

CHAPTER SUMMARY

Money

To buy something we need rupees or paise. These rupees and paise are called **money**. We see money in two forms (a) coins and (b) notes. Money is also known as **Currency**.

Important Points

(i) The Unit of currency in India is Rupees.

(ii) Symbol of Indian rupees is:

₹

(iii) Other important currencies in the world one USD $ (United States Dollar which is used in America), GBP (UK Pound Sterling) used in United Kingdom and Euro in Europe.

(iv) Money in India comes in form of paper as well as coins.

(v) 1 Rupee = 100 paise
10 coins of 10 paise make one Rupee.
2 coins of 50 paise make one Rupee.
4 coins of 25 paise make one Rupee.

1 coin of 50 paise and 2 coins of 25 paisa make one Rupee.

(vi) The paper based notes available in India are of ₹ 2000, ₹ 500, ₹ 200, ₹ 100, ₹ 50, ₹ 20, ₹ 10, ₹ 5 as shown ahead.

Notes (Paper Money) Currently in use in India

- Till few Year back there were paper notes for ₹ 2 and ₹ 1 as well but they are no longer in use but are still valid. Their picture is as shown below :

Coins Currently in use in India

- The coins available in India are of ₹ 10, ₹ 5, ₹ 2 and ₹ 1 as shown below :

Did You Know?

- Paper notes are called **bank notes** as they are issued by the Reserve Bank of India (RBI).

- Picture of Mahatma Gandhi, father of the nation, is printed on every note.
- Every note contains signature of RBI Governor.
- As the value of currency increases, the size of the paper note also increases.

TRIVIA

−40 degrees Celsius is similar to −40 degrees Fahrenheit.

Misconcept /Concept

Misconcept

If a paper note is mutilated or torn, then you feel that it cannot be used as no shopkeeper is ready to take it.

Concept

Torn or spoilt notes can be exchanged in banks and they will give you Money depending on the condition of the note.

MUST REMEMBER

➡ Money in India comes in form of paper as well as coins.
➡ Money is also known as Currency.
➡ Torn or spoilt notes can be exchanged in banks and they will give you Money depending on the condition of the note.

Direction (1–7) : Study the following information carefully and answer the following:

  (i)   Cost of dress = ₹ 30

  (ii) Cost of a pair of shoes = ₹ 19

  (iii) Cost of handbag = ₹ 59

  (iv) Cost of comb = ₹ 2

  (v) Cost of lipstick = ₹ 18

  (vi) Cost of mirror = ₹ 5

Shraddha goes shopping with ₹100.

1. A mirror cost ₹ _____ more than a comb.
    (a) 7   (b) 3
    (c) 2   (d) 5

2. A pair of shoes costs ₹ _____ less than a handbag.
    (a) 59+19   (b) 39
    (c) 59 – 19   (d) 49

3. Shraddha bought a dress and the lipstick. She spent ₹ _____ altogether.
    (a) 38   (b) 40
    (c) 45   (d) 48

4. If Shraddha buys a pair of shoes, a handbag and a mirror, she will spend ₹ _____.
    (a) 83   (b) 75
    (c) 66   (d) 84

5. If she buys a dress and a comb , she will have ₹ _____ left.
    (a) 57   (b) 36
    (c) 68   (d) 42

6. If Shraddha buys a handbag and another item, she will have ₹ 11 left. Other item she buys is _____.
    (a) Lipstick   (b) Dress
    (c) A pair of shoes (d) Mirror

7. After Shraddha bought two of the items, she has ₹ 63 left. What items did she buy?
    (a) Dress, mirror
    (b) Lipstick, mirror
    (c) A pair of shoes ,lipstick
    (d) Dress, comb

Direction (8–14) : Study the table below carefully and answer the following questions:

Item	Price
Eraser	25 paise
Correction pen	₹1
Ruler	50 paise
Exercise book	65 paise
Pen	₹2
Text book	₹4

8. Parveen wants to buy 2 erasers and 1 ruler. He needs _____ altogether.
    (a) 50 paise   (b) 75 paise
    (c) ₹ 1   (d) None of these

9. Kuku spent ₹ 10 to buy 2 textbook and a _____.
    (a) Correction pen   (b) Eraser
    (c) Ruler   (d) Pen

10. Anita bought 2 pens, 3 correction pens and a text book. She spend ₹ _____ altogether.
    (a) 11   (b) 9
    (c) 13   (d) 10

11. Vinay bought a textbook and he gave the cashier ₹ 10. He received ₹ ____ change.
    (a) 8   (b) 6
    (c) 4   (d) 2

12. Viru wants to buy an exercise book but he only has 45 paise. He will need _____ more.
    (a) 25 paise
    (b) 15 paise
    (c) 20 paise
    (d) 30 paise

13. Harish spent ₹ 10. He bought twice as many correction pens as rulers. He bought _____ correction pens and _____ ruler.
    (a) 6, 2
    (b) 6, 4
    (c) 8, 2
    (d) 8, 4

14. Mohit spent ₹ 10 to buy correction pens and rulers. He bought 4 more rulers than Harish. He bought _____ correction pens and _____ rulers.
    (a) 6, 8
    (b) 6, 4
    (c) 4, 6
    (d) 8, 4

15. The sum of five ₹ 10 notes and five ₹ 20 notes is _____.
    (a) ₹ 100
    (b) ₹ 150
    (c) ₹ 50
    (d) ₹ 200

16. How many ₹ 2 coins you need to make it ₹ 10?
    (a) 10
    (b) 4
    (c) 20
    (d) 5

17. What is the total of the following?

₹ 500

₹ 50

₹ 20

₹ 5

₹ 1

    (a) 550
    (b) 580
    (c) 576
    (d) 520

18. What does ₹ 9.35 mcan?
    (a) 9 rupees 35 paisa
    (b) 93 rupees 5 paisa
    (c) 935 rupees
    (d) None of these

19. What is the sum of ₹ 40.50 and ₹ 12.25?
    (a) ₹ 42.75
    (b) ₹ 52.75
    (c) ₹ 50.25
    (d) ₹ 52.25

20. How much more money you need to make ₹ 112.25 as ₹ 245.75?
    (a) ₹ 130.50
    (b) ₹ 133.50
    (c) ₹ 133.40
    (d) ₹ 133

21. XYZ shopping centre is having a half-price sale. A T-shirt which originally costs ₹ 10 is now going of ₹ 5. How many T-shirts can now be bought for ₹ 30?
    (a) 7
    (b) 6
    (c) 5
    (d) 8

22. Leela had 3 fifty-rupee notes, 2 ten rupee notes and 5 two- rupee notes. After she treated her family to dinner, she had ₹ 65 left. How much did the dinner cost?
    (a) ₹ 85
    (b) ₹ 110
    (c) ₹ 115
    (d) ₹ 95

23. Price of some vegetables are _____.

Tomato   – ₹ 10 per kg

Capsicum – ₹ 15 per kg

Cucumber – ₹ 20 per kg

If Shradha bought 2 kg of tomatoes 1 kg capsicum and 2 kg cucumber, how much she paid in total?

(a) ₹ 80   (b) ₹ 20

(c) ₹ 75   (d) ₹ 100

24. Rita has ₹ 200. She gave ₹ 50 to her friend. How much money she has now?

(a) ₹ 75   (b) ₹ 50

(c) ₹ 100   (d) ₹ 150

25. Soma purchased a doll for ₹ 540 and a ring for ₹ 220. What is that total amount spent by her?

(a) ₹ 740   (b) ₹ 750

(c) ₹ 760   (d) ₹ 770

HOTS

1. Nisha has ₹ 600. She purchased the following items;

   2 flower bouquets for ₹ 100

   A doll for ₹ 100

   4 notebooks, each for ₹ 50

   How much money is left with her after shopping?

   (a) ₹ 100   (b) ₹ 150

   (c) ₹ 200   (d) ₹ 150

2. Aman has 3 hundred rupee notes 2 fifty rupee notes and 5 five rupees notes, he spent ₹ 255 on shopping. How much money is left with him now?

   (a) ₹ 180   (b) ₹ 170

   (c) ₹ 200   (d) ₹ 250

3. Preeti has ₹ 500. If she bought 25 oranges each for ₹ 9. Which expression shows the correct amount of change that she will get back?

   (a) $500 + 25$ (b) $500 + 25 \times 9$

   (c) $500 - 25 \times 9$ (d) $500 \times 25 + 9$

4. Ricky opened up his piggy bank to buy a robot of Rs. 200. In her piggy bank she found 10 coins of Rs. 10, 9 coins ₹ 5 and 5 coins of ₹ 2. How much more money does she need to buy robot?

   (a) ₹ 50   (b) ₹ 60

   (c) ₹ 40   (d) ₹ 45

5. A family went to a mall. They spent Rs. 70 on ice-cream, Rs. 85 on balloons and Rs. 155 for tickets of a drama. How much did the family spend at the mall?

   (a) ₹ 310   (b) ₹ 300

   (c) ₹ 350   (d) ₹ 410

1. Sheela bought a dress for 250 and a bag for Rs. 150. How much money the shopkeeper returned, if Sheela gave him a note of Rs. 500?

   Answer:

   Total amount spent on items = ₹ 250 + ₹ 150 = ₹ 400

   Amount returned by the shopkeeper = ₹ 500 – ₹ 400 = ₹ 100

2. Shalu has 7 twenty rupees note. How much money he has?

   Answer:

   7 twenty rupees = 7 × 20 = 140 rupees

   Hence, Shalu has ₹ 140 with her.

3. The cost of 2 metre nylon cloth is ₹ 25 and 2 metre cotton cloth is ₹ 30. What is the cost of 4 metre nylon and 4 metre cotton cloth together?

   Answer:

   Cost of 2 metre nylon = ₹ 25

   Cost of 4 metre nylon = 2 × ₹ 25 = ₹ 50

   Cost of 2 metre cotton ₹ 30

   Cost of 4 metre cotton = 2×30 = ₹ 60

   Cost of 4metre nylon and 4 metre cotton = ₹60 + 50 = ₹110

4. Ashish went to the market with ₹ 200. He bought mangoes for ₹ 50 and notebooks for ₹ 100. How much money is he left with after spending?

   Solution:

   Total money he had = ₹ 200

   Cost of mangoes = ₹ 50

   Cost of notebooks = ₹ 100

   Total amount he spend = ₹ (100 + 50) = ₹ 150

   Money he is left with = ₹ (200 – 150) = ₹ 50.

Geometrical Shapes

8

Learning Objectives : In this chapter, students will learn about:
- ✓ Point and Line
- ✓ Types of Line
- ✓ Plane Shapes
- ✓ Solid Shapes

CHAPTER SUMMARY

Geometry
Geometry is the study of angles, lines and their relationships with each other.

Straight Line
If we stretch a thread tightly we get a straight line.

Curved Line
If we hold the thread loosely, we get a curved line.

Squares, rectangles and triangles are made of straight lines.

Circles and ovals are made of curved lines.

Horizontal, Vertical and Slanting Lines
A straight line can be horizontal, vertical or slanting.

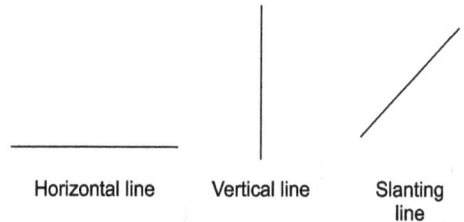

Horizontal line   Vertical line   Slanting line

Plane Shapes
Circles, triangles, squares, rectangles and ovals are called flat or **plane shapes**.

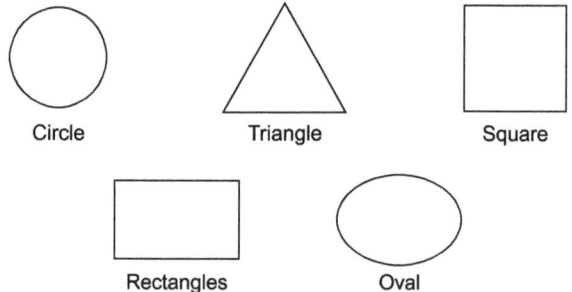

Circle   Triangle   Square

Rectangles   Oval

Triangle : A triangle has three sides, and three corners.

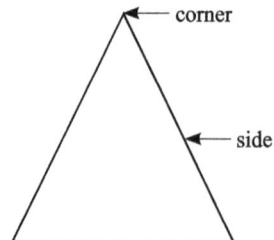

corner

side

Square : A square has 4 sides and 4 corners. All its sides have the same length.

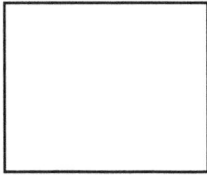

Rectangle : A rectangle has 4 sides, 2 diagonals and 4 corners. Its opposite sides have the same length.

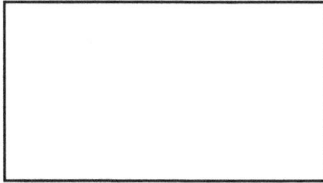

Circle : A circle has no side and corner.

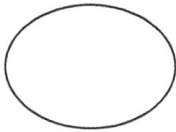

Oval : An oval has no sides or corners.

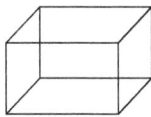

Solid Shapes

Cube, cuboid, cylinder, sphere and cone are all solid shapes.

Cube   Cuboid

Cylinder   Sphere   Cone

Cuboid : It has six flat faces.
It has 8 corners and 12 edges.

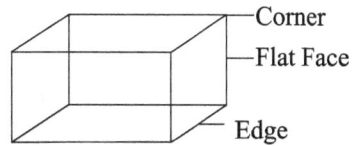

Corner
Flat Face
Edge

Cube : It has six equal flat faces. It has 8 corners and 12 edges.

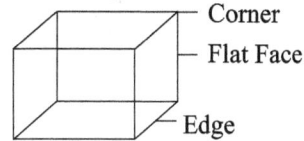

Corner
Flat Face
Edge

Cylinder : It has 2 edge, 3 faces and no corner. It has two flat faces and one curved face.

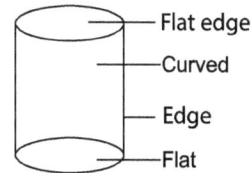

Flat edge
Curved
Edge
Flat

Sphere : It has only one curved face. It has no edge and corner.

Curved

Cone : It has one flat face and one curved face.

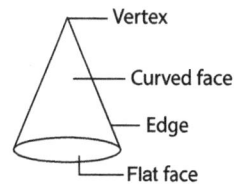

Vertex
Curved face
Edge
Flat face

TRIVIA

The hour and minute hand of a clock coincide 22 times in a day.

➡ Geometry is the study of angles, lines and their relationships with each other.

➡ Squares, rectangles and triangles are made of straight lines.

1. How many triangles are there in the given figure?

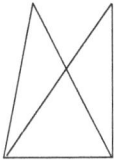

   (a) 3   (b) 5
   (c) 2   (d) 6

2. How many slanting lines are there in the given figure?

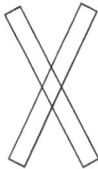

   (a) 6   (b) 8
   (c) 2   (d) 4

3. Number of curved lines in the given figure is _____.

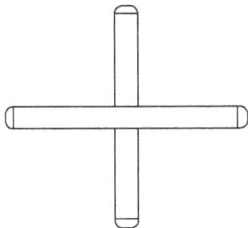

   (a) 4   (b) 8
   (c) 10   (d) None of these

4. How many edges are these in the given figure?

   (a) 8   (b) 5
   (c) 10   (d) 9

5. Out of given figures, which figure has maximum number of edges.

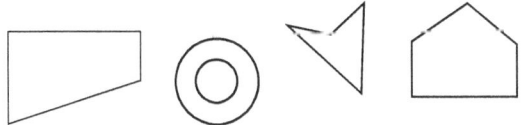

     (i)   (ii)   (iii)   (iv)

   (a) ii   (b) iii
   (c) iv   (d) i

6. Given line is _____ .

   (a) Curved   (b) Slant
   (c) Straight   (d) None of these

7. Count the vertical lines in the given figure.

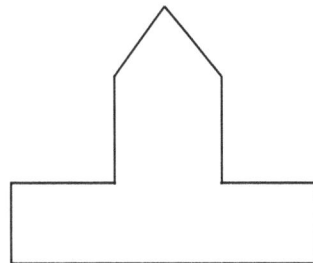

   (a) 1   (b) 2
   (c) 3   (d) 4

8. The line | is_____.

   (a) Slant   (b) Curved
   (c) Vertical   (d) None of these

9. The line / is _____ .

   (a) Slant   (b) Curved
   (c) Straight   (d) None of these

Direction (10–11) : See the given figure and and answer the questions

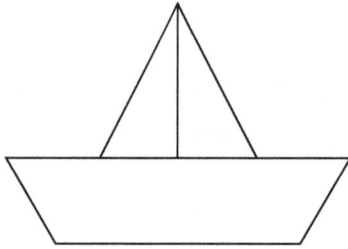

10. Count the slanting lines in the figure.
    (a) 4   (b) 3
    (c) 6   (d) 5

11. Count the total lines in the figure.
    (a) 6   (b) 7
    (c) 5   (d) 8

12. A rectangle has _____ sides.
    (a) 2   (b) 4
    (c) 6   (d) 0

13. A square has _____ corners.
    (a) 4   (b) 6
    (c) 2   (d) 0

14. A rectangle has _____ corners.
    (a) 4   (b) 6
    (c) 2   (d) 0

15. An oval has _____ sides.
    (a) 0   (b) 1
    (c) 2   (d) 3

16. A cube has _____ flat faces.
    (a) 6   (b) 4
    (c) 2   (d) 8

17. A cone has _____ curved face.
    (a) 1   (b) 2
    (c) 3   (d) 4

18. Flat face of a cube is a _____ .
    (a) Square   (b) Rectangle
    (c) Oval   (d) Triangle

19. Match the shaded face of objects with the correct shape.

A.		1.	
B.		2.	
C.		3.	
D.		4.	

Codes

	A	B	C	D
a.	1	2	3	4
b.	3	4	2	1
c.	2	1	3	4
d.	3	4	1	2

20. What is the shape of base of a cylinder?
    (a) Circle   (b) Square
    (c) Rectangle   (d) None of these

21. Naina has 5 matchsticks. She made a design with these matchsticks. Which of the following is the possible design made by her, if her design has two slanting, two standing and one sleeping line?
    (a)   (b)
    (c)   (d) None of these

22. Rohan wants to make a cube shaped box. How many squares he needs to make the box?
    (a) 5   (b) 6
    (c) 7   (d) 4

23. Santa has to make a model of a rocket. Which two shapes he needs two make the following model?

    (a) Cone and cube
    (b) Sphere and cone
    (c) Cone and cylinder
    (d) None of these

24. Sohan has some erasers.

    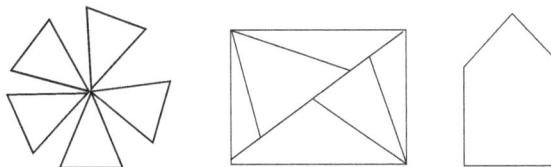

    These are _____ lines in the erasers altogether.
    (a) 31   (b) 29
    (c) 30   (d) 32

25. If Neha places some rectangles above the other, then which shape she will get?
    (a) Cone   (b) Sphere
    (c) Cube   (d) Cuboid

HOTS

1. Shape _____ has largest number of sides.

   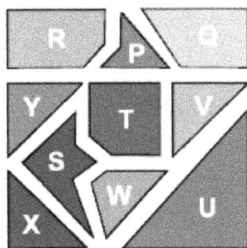

   (a) T   (b) R
   (c) S   (d) P

2. Look at the given shapes.

   Which statement is correct?

   (i) All the shapes are made up of straight lines.
   (ii) All the shapes have up exactly four lines.
   (iii) All the shapes are made of curved lines.
   (a) (i)   (b) (ii)
   (c) (iii)   (d) Both (i) and (ii)

3. How many ⬡ are there in given figures?

   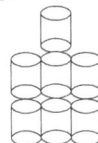

   (a) 7   (b) 12
   (c) 10   (d) None of these

4. Count the triangles.

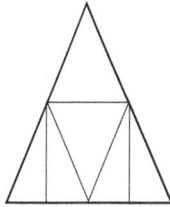

(a) 5   (b) 10

(c) 9   (d) 12

5. Identify the figure.
   I have two circular faces and one curved face. I have no corners. Soft drink cans often look like me. Who am I?
   (a) Cuboid   (b) Cylinder
   (c) Cone   (d) Cube

SUBJECTIVE QUESTIONS

1. How many sides and corners does the following shapes have?

   (i) Triangle   (ii) Square

   (iii) Rectangle   (iv) Circle

   Answer:

Shapes	Sides	Corners
Triangle	3	3
Square	4	4
Rectangle	4	4
Circles	0	0

2. What are Decreasing and Repeating patterns?

   Answer:

   Decreasing Pattern:

   In decreasing pattern numbers decrease in a certain manner, for example.

   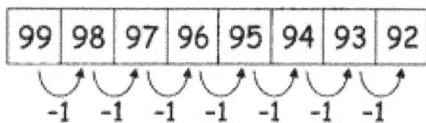

   In the above example numbers are decreasing by one.

   Repeating Pattern:

   In repeating pattern numbers are repeated in a certain manner, for example.

   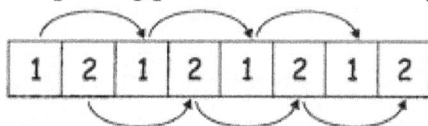

   In the above example 1 and 2 are appearing one by one.

3. Highlight the shape which best matches the real life object in the pictures given below.

(a)

Cone / Cube / Cylinder	Cone / Sphere / Cylinder	Cylinder / Cone / Cube

(b)

Cone / Cube / Cylinder	Sphere / Cube / Cylinder	Cone / Sphere / Cylinder

(c)

Cone / Sphere / Cylinder	Cone / Cube / Cylinder	Sphere / Cone / Cube

Answer:

(a)

Cone / Cube / Cylinder	Cone / **Sphere** / Cylinder	**Cylinder** / Cone / Cube

(b)		

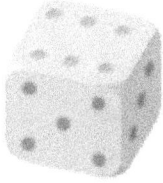

Cone / **Cube** / Cylinder	Sphere / Cube / **Cylinder**	**Cone** / Sphere / Cylinder

(c)		

Cone / Sphere / Cylinder	Cone / **Cube** / Cylinder	**Sphere** / Cone / Cube

Pictographs

Learning Objectives : In this chapter, students will learn about:
- ✓ Pictographs

CHAPTER SUMMARY

Pictographs

Pictures that represent information are called **pictographs**. A pictograph uses pictures or symbols to represent an assigned amount of data. It is a useful method to represent data attractively.

Numerical data when presented through pictures is called **pictorial representation**.

Pictographs are also called as pictograms.

Examples: The picture graph below shows the groceries Navneet bought for his restaurant in January. Study the graph and answer the given questions.

Groceries Navneet bought in January					
Rice	🏺	🏺	🏺	🏺	🏺 🏺
Sugar	🏺	🏺	🏺		
Flour	🏺	🏺	🏺	🏺	
Barley	🏺	🏺			
Oats	🏺	🏺	🏺		

Each 🏺 stands for 4 kg.

> **TRIVIA**
>
> The word love in tennis means a score of zero.

1 : Navneet bought _____ kg of rice.
- (a) 16
- (b) 12
- (c) 24
- (d) 8

Solution : (c) Navneet bought $4 \times 6 = 24$ kg of rice.

2 : He bought 16 kg of _____.
- (a) Rice
- (b) Flour
- (c) Oats
- (d) Sugar

Solution : (c) Navneet bought $4 \times 4 = 16$ kg of flour.

3 : He bought _____ fewer kilograms of barley than rice.
- (a) 4
- (b) 20
- (c) 8
- (d) 16

Solution : (d) Required weight = weight of rice − weight of barley

$$= 4 \times 6 - 4 \times 2$$

$$= 24 - 8 = 16$$

4 : He bought _____ kg of oats and sugar altogether.

    (a) 24   (b) 16

    (c) 8   (d) 6

Solution : (a) Required weight of oats + weight of sugar $= 4 \times 3 + 4 \times 3$

$$= 12 + 12 = 24 \text{ kg}$$

5 : Each kilogram of barley cost ₹ 2. He paid ₹ _____ for the barley altogether.

    (a) 4   (b) 16

    (c) 12   (d) 24

Solution : (b) Navneet paid $= 4 \times 2 \times 2 = ₹ 16$

6 : Navneet spent ₹ 12 on oats. Each kilogram on oats costs ₹ _____.

    (a) 12   (b) 4

    (c) 3   (d) 1

Solution : (d) Weight of oats $= 4 \times 3 = 12$ kg

$$\therefore \text{ Required cost } = \frac{12}{12} = 1$$

MUST REMEMBER

➡ Pictures that represent information are called pictographs. A pictograph uses pictures or symbols to represent an assigned amount of data.

1. If △ stands for 4, then △△△△△ stands for _____.
   (a) 10   (b) 13
   (c) 20   (d) 16

2. If ▤ stands for 3, then ▤▤▤ stands for ___.
   (a) 9   (b) 10
   (c) 11   (d) 12

3. If ▽ stands for 2, then ▽▽ stands for _____.
   (a) 2   (b) 4
   (c) 6   (d) 8

4. If 🐢 🐢 🐢 🐢 🐢 stands for 25, then 🐢 stands for _____.
   (a) 8   (b) 6
   (c) 5   (d) 10

5. If △△△△ stands for 40, then △△ stands for _____
   (a) 20   (b) 10
   (c) 15   (d) 25

Direction (6–9) : The picture graph below shows the number of cookies 5 children ate. Study the graph and answer the given questions.

Number of cookies each child ate	
Ram	🍪🍪🍪🍪🍪
Aman	🍪🍪
Sumit	🍪🍪🍪
Karan	🍪🍪🍪🍪
Aayush	🍪🍪🍪🍪🍪🍪🍪

Each 🍪 stands for 3

6. _____ ate the most number of cookies.
   (a) Aayush   (b) Ram
   (c) Karan   (d) Sumit

7. Sumit ate _____ cookies.
   (a) 3   (b) 6
   (c) 9   (d) 12

8. _____ and _____ ate 18 cookies altogether.
   (a) Ram, Sumit   (b) Aman, Karan
   (c) Aman, Sumit   (d) Ram, Aman

9. _____ ate 6 cookies more than B.
   (a) Ram   (b) Aman
   (c) Aayush   (d) None of these

Direction (10–12): The picture graph below shows favourite pastimes of a group of children. Study the graph and answer the given questions.

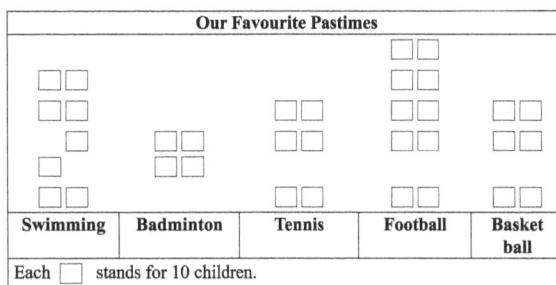

Our Favourite Pastimes				
Swimming	Badminton	Tennis	Football	Basket ball

Each ☐ stands for 10 children.

10. If 45 boys like swimming, _____ girls like swimming.
    (a) 45   (b) 35
    (c) 25   (d) Can't say

11. _____ is the most popular pastime.

(a) Badminton   (b) Tennis

(c) Football   (d) Basket ball

12. If the same number of boys and girls like basket ball, _____ boys like basket ball.

(a) 100   (b) 80

(c) 60   (d) 30

Direction (13–14) : Use the information below to answer the given questions.

Number of mobile phones sold by Mr. Sharma	
Thursday	
Friday	
Saturday	
Sunday	
Each stands for 3 mobile phones.	

13. He sold _____ mobile phones on Saturday and Sunday.

(a) 16   (b) 48

(c) 75   (d) 80

14. If he sold 3 more mobile phones on Friday, he would have sold as many mobile phones as on _____.

(a) Thursday   (b) Saturday

(c) Sunday   (d) None of these

Direction (15–18) : The King's Fun Fair is in town! Children played the games to win tokens and exchange for toys. Read the following information and answer the questions.

Each ⬤ stands for 2 tokens.

15. Shraddha won 10 tokens at the fun fair. She needed _____ more tokens to exchange for a toy robot.

(a) 1   (b) 2

(c) 3   (d) 4

16. Golu won twice as many tokens as Shraddha.

He could get the _____ .

(a) Robot   (b) Teddy bear

(c) Toy gun   (d) Mini computer

17. Jasmine had just enough tokens to exchange for a teddy bear. If she wanted to exchange her tokens for a 2 toy aeroplanes, she will need _____ more tokens.

(a) 8   (b) 6

(c) 4   (d) 2

18. Krishna won 30 tokens. He exchanged all of them for two toys. He chose the _____ and the _____ .

(a) Toy gun, toy plane

(b) Robot, teddy bear

(c) Robot, mini computer

(d) Teddy bear, mini computer

Direction : Look at the picture graph and answer the question.

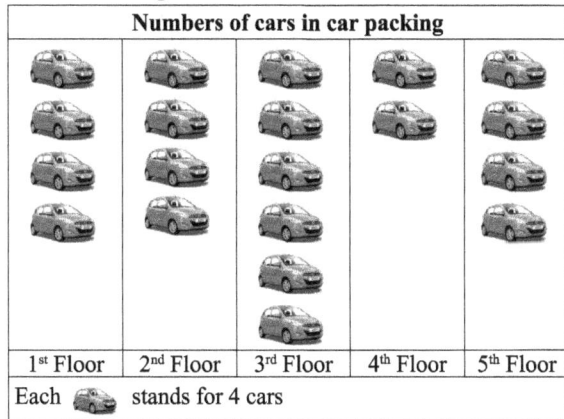

Numbers of cars in car packing				
1st Floor	2nd Floor	3rd Floor	4th Floor	5th Floor

Each 🚗 stands for 4 cars

19. There were _____ more cars parked on 3rd floor than on the 5th floor.
    (a) 4   (b) 8
    (c) 32   (d) 12

Direction (20–22) : Naina decided to plant trees. So she planted trees for four days.

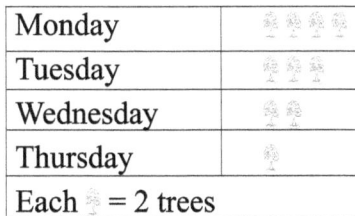

Monday	🌳🌳🌳🌳
Tuesday	🌳🌳🌳
Wednesday	🌳🌳
Thursday	🌳
Each 🌳 = 2 trees	

Using given information, answer the following.

20. How many tress were planted on Wednesday?
    (a) 8   (b) 10
    (c) 2   (d) 4

21. How many trees were planted on second day?
    (a) 6   (b) 4
    (c) 8   (d) 12

22. How many more trees were planted on Monday than Tuesday?
    (a) 4   (b) 2
    (c) 20   (d) 7

Direction (23–25) : The pictograph shows the number of stickers achieved by four children in a week. Study the graph and answer the following questions.

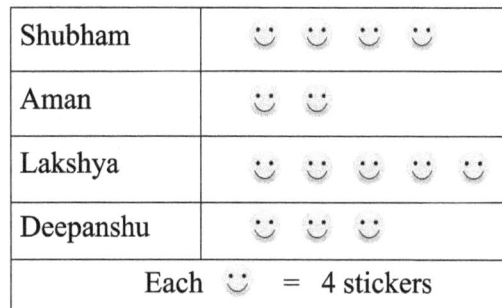

Shubham	☺ ☺ ☺ ☺
Aman	☺ ☺
Lakshya	☺ ☺ ☺ ☺ ☺
Deepanshu	☺ ☺ ☺
Each ☺ = 4 stickers	

23. Who got maximum stickers?
    (a) Shubham   (b) Aman
    (c) Lakshya   (d) Deepanshu

24. Shubham got _____ more stickers than Aman.
    (a) 8   (b) 10
    (c) 9   (d) 15

25. Aman and Deepanshu got _____ stickers altogether.
    (a) 15   (b) 20
    (c) 10   (d) 25

1. Ankit makes pictograph of the number of toys his friends have. How many less toys Kriti has than the total number of toys 3 friends have?

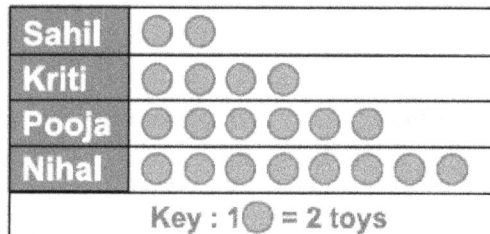

Sahil	◖◖
Kriti	◖◖◖
Pooja	◖◖◖◖◖
Nihal	◖◖◖◖◖◖

Key : 1◖ = 2 toys

(a) 20 (b) 32
(c) 24 (d) 26

2. The picture graph shows the number of students present from Monday to Friday.

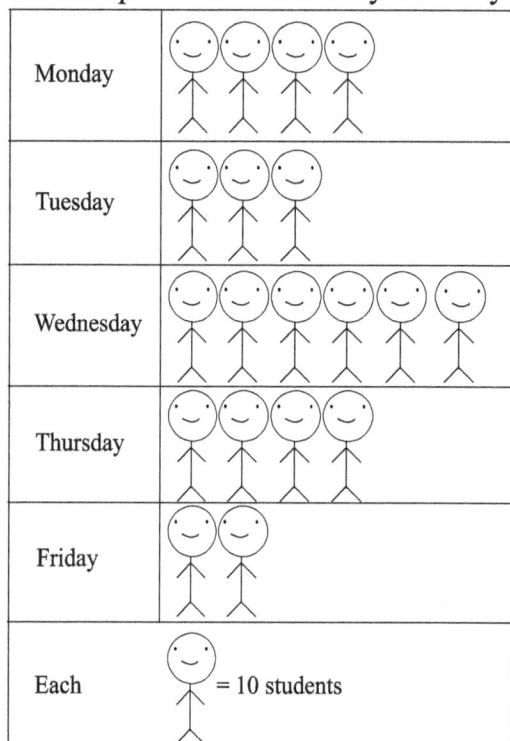

Monday	😊😊😊😊
Tuesday	😊😊😊
Wednesday	😊😊😊😊😊😊
Thursday	😊😊😊😊
Friday	😊😊
Each	😊 = 10 students

How many more students were present on Wednesday than Friday?
(a) 40 (b) 50
(c) 45 (d) 35

3. If 😊 + 😊 + 😊 + 😊 = 400 and 😄 + 😄 = 500, then 😊 + 😄 = ?
(a) 150 (b) 250
(c) 300 (d) 350

4. The picture graph shows the numbers of pencils purchased by 4 children.

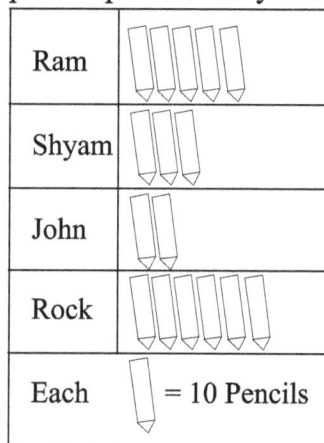

Ram	✏✏✏✏
Shyam	✏✏
John	✏
Rock	✏✏✏✏✏
Each	✏ = 10 Pencils

If the cost of one pencil is ₹10. How much will Ram have to pay for his pencils?
(a) 300 (b) 400
(c) 500 (d) 600

5. The following pictograph shows the number of balls purchased by 4 girls.

Sony	⚾⚾⚾⚾
Nisha	⚾⚾⚾
Priya	⚾
Jyoti	⚾⚾⚾
1 ⚾	= 5 Balls

Using the given information, find out which of the following statements is incorrect?

(a) Sony purchased maximum balls.

(b) Priya purchased 10 balls.

(c) Nisha and Jyoti purchased the same number of balls.

(d) Nisha purchased 5 less balls than Sony.

SUBJECTIVE QUESTIONS

1. If 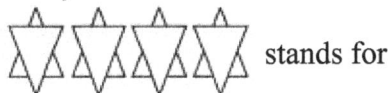 stands for 3, then

stands for

Answer:

= 3

So,

= 3 + 3 + 3 + 3 = 12

2. If  stands for 12, then

stands for

Answer:

 = 12

= 12 + 12 + 12 = 36

3. The picture graph given shows the number of eggs collected by a farmer on 5 different days.

Monday	Tuesday	Wednesday	Thursday	Friday

Each ◯ stands for 5 eggs.

How many more eggs were collected on Thursday than on Monday?

Answer:

No. of eggs collected on Thursday

= 8 × 5 = 40

No. of eggs collected on Tuesday

= 6 × 5 = 30

Therefore, there difference is 10. Hence, 10 more eggs were collected on Thursday than Monday.

4. The given pictograph shows the number of students in each section of class 2. Study the graph and answer the following question:

2-A	☺☺☺☺
2-B	☺☺☺
2-C	☺☺☺
2-D	☺☺☺☺☺
Each ☺ stands for 5 students	

How many total number of students are there in class 2?

Answer:

Number of students in class 2 – A = 20
Number of students in class 2 – B = 15
Number of students in class 2 – C = 15
Number of students in class 2 – D = 25
Total number of students in class 2 = 20 + 15 + 15 + 25 = 75

5. The picture graph shows the types of colours various children prefer. Study the graph and answer the following questions.

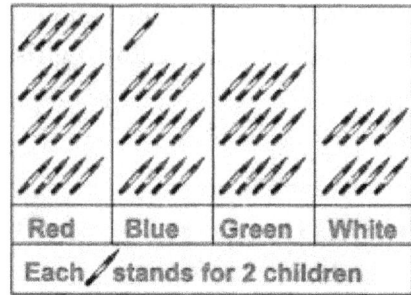

Red	Blue	Green	White
Each ╱ stands for 2 children			

How many children prefer green and white colour altogether?

Answer:

Number of children who prefer green colour = 24

Number of children who prefer white colour = 16

Therefore, Number of children who prefer green and white colour together = 24 + 16 = 40

🕐🕐🕐

SECTION 2
LOGICAL REASONING

Patterns

Learning Objectives : In this chapter, students will learn about:
- ✓ Concept of Pattern

CHAPTER SUMMARY

You can use a pattern to decide which shape comes next in a design. Look at the design and find the repeated pattern.

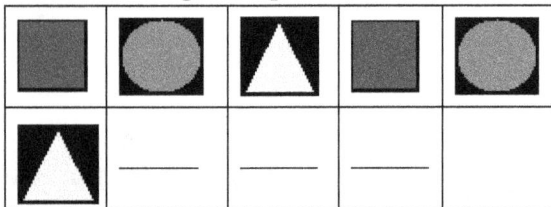

What are the next three shapes in the pattern? The pattern is : square, circle, triangle; square, circle, triangle. So the next three shapes in the pattern are :

You can use patterns to decide what numbers come next in a design with a series of numbers. Look at star A. Point number 1 has a value of 4. Go to the next point and look for a number pattern in the star.

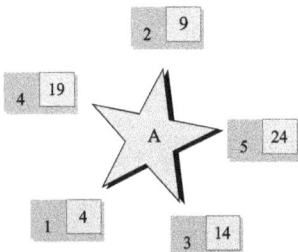

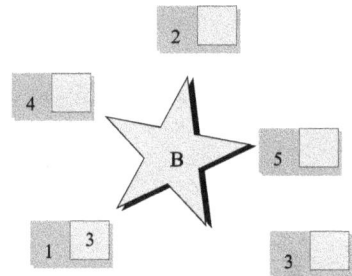

What is the difference between each number? Each number is 5 more than the one before it. The first point is 4.

The second is 9.

The third is 14.

The fourth is 19.

The fifth is 24.

Use the same number pattern to find the next four numbers in star B. Start with the first point as 3 and add 5 each time to get the next number. They should be 8, 13, 18, 23.

You can use patterns to decide what numbers come next in a series of numbers.

Example :

Look for a number pattern.

$$2, 5, 8, 11, \_\_, \_\_, \_\_$$

What is the difference between each number?

Solution: Each number is 3 more than the one before it. Use the number pattern to find the next three numbers.

$$11+3 = 14 \quad 14+3 = 17 \quad 17+3 = 20$$

→ 2, 5, 8, 11, 14, 17, 20

Example :

Look for a number pattern.

11, 9, 7, __, __, __,

What is the difference between the numbers?

Solution: Each number is 2 less than the number before. Use the number pattern to find the next three numbers.

$$11 - 2 = 9 \quad 9 - 2 = 7 \quad 7 - 2 = 5$$

$$5 - 2 = 3 \quad 3 - 2 = 1$$

11, 9, 7, 5, 3, 1

You can use number patterns to complete a table. The number pattern is the rule for the table.

IN	2	3	4	5	9	10
OUT	5	6	7			

So, what is the rule? What do you have to do to each IN number to get the OUT number below it?

$$2 + 3 = 5 \quad 3 + 3 = 6 \quad 4 + 3 = 7$$

You add 3 to each IN number to get the OUT number. The rule for this table is Add 3. Use the rule to complete the table.

IN	2	3	4	5	9	10
OUT	5	6	7	8	12	13

Example: Find the number pattern to complete the table.

IN	11	10	9	5	7	6
OUT	7	6	5			

Solution: Here, you subtract 4 from each IN number to get the OUT number.

$$11 - 4 = 7 \quad 10 - 4 = 6 \quad 9 - 4 = 5$$

The rule for this table is subtract 4. Thus,

IN	11	10	9	5	7	6
OUT	7	6	5	1	3	2

1. What are the next two shapes to complete the pattern?

   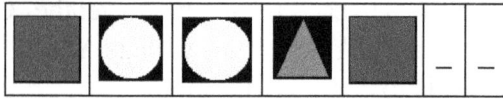

   (a) Circle, circle
   (b) Triangle, circle
   (c) Circle, triangle
   (d) Square, circle

2. What are the next two shapes to complete the pattern?

   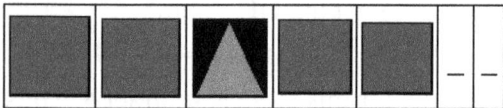

   (a) Circle, circle
   (b) Triangle, square
   (c) Circle, triangle
   (d) Square, circle

3. Find the number pattern in star A. The first point has a value of 3. Then look at star B. Use the same number pattern to figure out the value of the other points.

   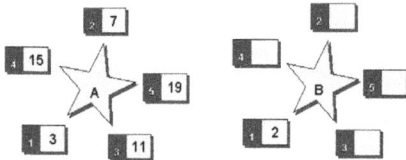

   (a) 5, 7, 9, 18
   (b) 4, 6, 8, 10
   (c) 6, 10, 14, 18
   (d) 10, 12, 14, 16

4. What number should be on the other points of star B if you follow the same pattern?

   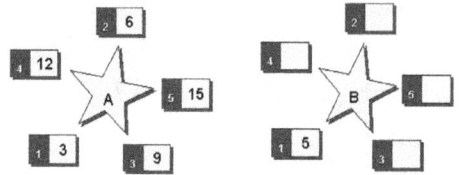

   (a) 5, 7, 9, 18
   (b) 8, 11, 15, 17
   (c) 6, 10, 14, 18
   (d) 10, 15, 20, 25

5. Write the next 3 numbers in the pattern.
   30, 32, 34, ___, ___, ___
   (a) 36, 38, 40   (b) 34, 36, 38
   (c) 36, 40, 44   (d) None of these

6. Write the next 3 numbers in the pattern.
   5, 10, 15, ___, ___, ___
   (a) 25, 30, 35   (b) 20, 25, 30
   (c) 25, 35, 45   (d) 20, 30, 40

7. Write the next 3 numbers in the pattern.
   27, 24, 21, ___, ___, ___
   (a) 15, 12, 10   (b) 20, 19, 18
   (c) 18, 15, 12   (d) None of these

8. Write the next 3 numbers in the pattern.
   24, 20, 16, ___, ___, ___
   (a) 10, 8, 6   (b) 4, 6, 8
   (c) 6, 10, 14   (d) 12, 8, 4

9. Write the numbers to complete the table given below.

IN	2	3	4	5	8	10
OUT	4	5	6			

   (a) 7, 10, 12   (b) 4, 6, 8
   (c) 6, 10, 14   (d) 12, 8, 4

10. Write the numbers to complete the table given below.

IN	4	5	6	7	9	10
OUT	8	9	10			

(a) 10, 8, 6
(b) 11, 13, 14
(c) 6, 10, 14
(d) 12, 8, 4

11. Find the letter which will end the first word and start the second word.

MA?ET

(a) K
(b) T
(c) N
(d) L

12. Find the rule followed in the figure pattern and missing figure.

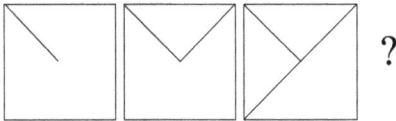

(a)
(b)
(c)
(d)

13. Which of the following replaces the question mark (?) so that figure series is formed?

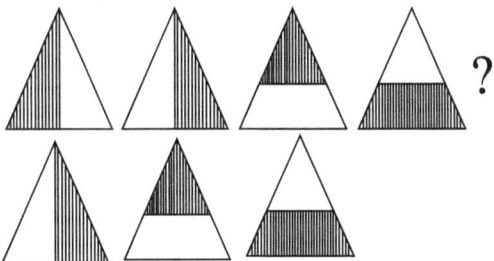

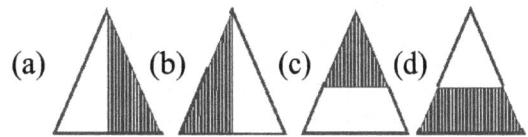

(a)
(b)
(c)
(d)

14. Which is the next letter?

D B A C   D B A C   D B A C   D B - -

(a) DB
(b) CD
(c) AC
(d) BA

15. How many triangles will be there in pattern 4?

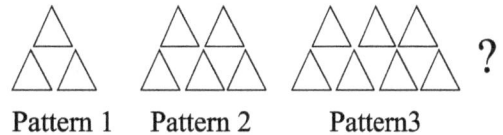

Pattern 1   Pattern 2   Pattern 3

(a) 9
(b) 10
(c) 11
(d) 12

16. In which of the following figure, Shape (X) is exactly embedded?

Shape (X)

(a)
(b)
(c)
(d)

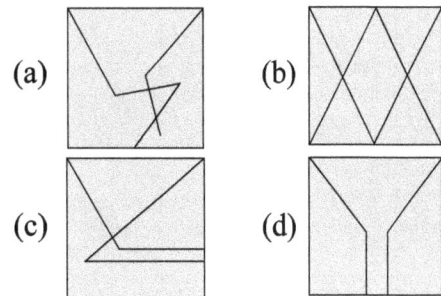

17. Find P and Q respectively.

(a)
(b)
(c)
(d)

18. Find the missing clock if given pattern is followed on the clocks.

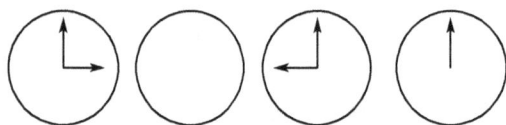

(a)   (b)

(c)   (d)

19. Which of the following figures will complete the pattern in figure (x)?

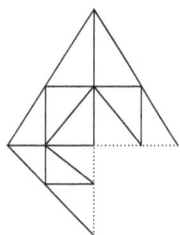

figure (x)

(a)   (b)   (c)   (d)

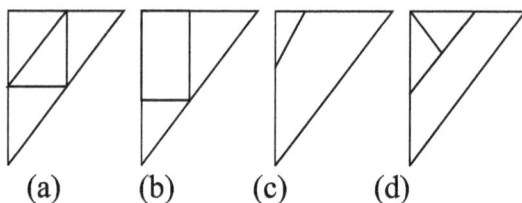

20. How many pencils will be there in pattern 4 ?

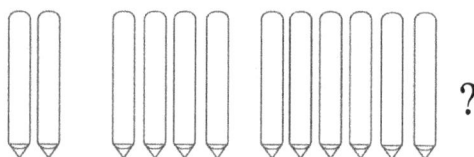

Pattern 1   Pattern 2   Pattern 3

(a) 14   (b) 12
(c) 8   (d) 16

Analogy

2

CHAPTER SUMMARY

In analogy, there is a certain connection between each given pair of figures. We have to find out the relation of the given pair and also find the missing figure.

Example: Identify the relation to find the missing figure.

(a)   (b)

(c)   (d)

Answer: (c)

Explanation: Outer shape of the first figure becomes inner shape of the second figure.

MULTIPLE CHOICE QUESTIONS

Direction: There is a certain rule between the pair of figure on the left side of : : Identify it and then find the missing figure.

1.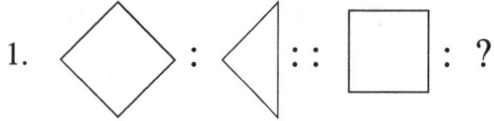

    (a)   (b)

    (c)   (d)

2.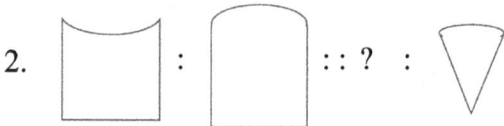

    (a)   (b)

    (c)   (d)

3.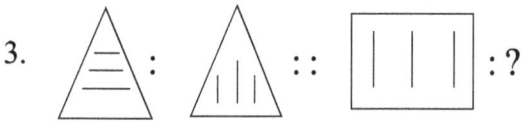

    (a)   (b)

    (c)   (d)

4.

    (a)   (b)

    (c)   (d)

5.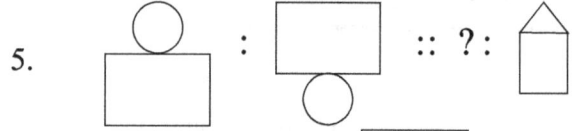

    (a)   (b)

    (c)   (d)

6.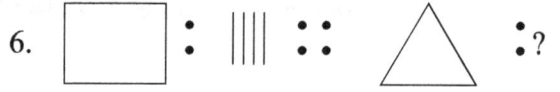

    (a) | (b) ||
    (c) ||| (d) ||||

7.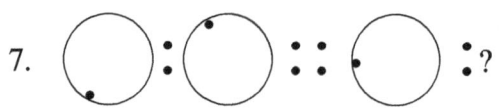

    (a)   (b)

    (c)   (d)

8.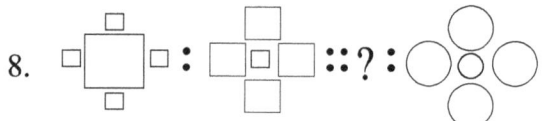

    (a)   (b)   (c)   (d)

9.

    (a)   (b)   (c)   (d)

10.

(a)   (b)

(c)   (d)

11.

(a)   (b)   (c)   (d)

12.

(a)   (b)   (c)   (d)

13.

(a)   (b)   (c)   (d)

14.

(a)   (b)   (c)   (d)

15.

(a)   (b)   (c)   (d)

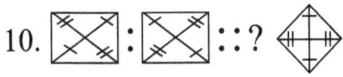

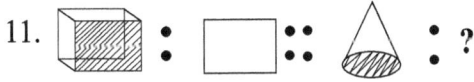

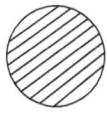

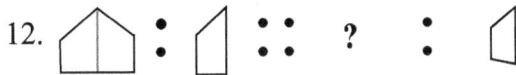

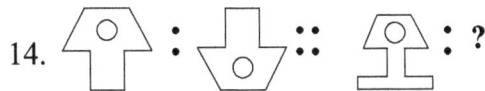

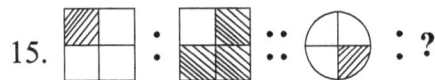

Direction (16–20) : There is a relation between figure (i) and (iii) and (ii) and (iv). Find the missing figure.

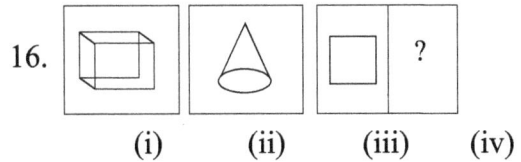

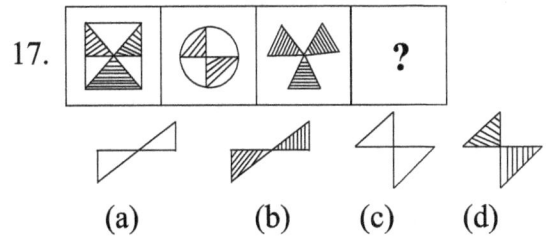

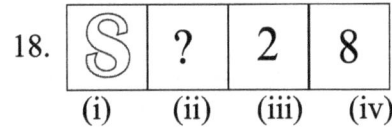

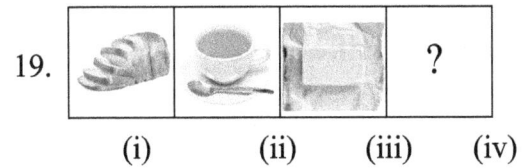

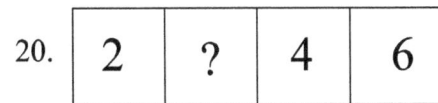

16.

(i)   (ii)   (iii)   (iv)

(a)   (b)   (c)   (d)

17.

(a)   (b)   (c)   (d)

18.

(i)	(ii)	(iii)	(iv)
S	?	2	8

(i)   (ii)   (iii)   (iv)

P   T   V   D

(a)   (b)   (c)   (d)

19.

(i)   (ii)   (iii)   (iv)

(a)   (b)   (c)   (d)

20.

2	?	4	6

   (i)   (ii)   (iii)   (iv)

(a) 11   (b) 3

(c) 5   (d) 1

Classification

3

CHAPTER SUMMARY

Classification (Odd One Out)

Classification test which is popularly known as 'Odd Man Out' test requires assorting of the items of a given group on the basis of a certain common quality they possess and then spotting the odd one in the group.

In this type of questions out of 3-4 objects (may be letters, words, numbers or figures) all but one are similar in some respect. We have to sort out which one is different. (*i.e.*, does not bear the same characteristics as the others in the given group.)

Types of Classification

(i) **Alphabet/Letter Classification :** In this type we have to identify an alphabet or a group of alphabets that are different from other given items.

(ii) **Number Classification**

(iii) **Word Classification**

Example : Find odd one out.
   (a) N   (b) M
   (c) I   (d) E

Solution : (a) Except N, any other has odd place value in the English alphabet.

Example: Three of the following four are alike in same way and so form a group. Which is one that does not belong to that group?
   (a) 37   (b) 48
   (c) 59   (d) 38

Solution : (d) Except 38, in all other number, difference between two digits is 4.

Direction (1–20) : In each of the following questions choose the one which is different from the others.

1. (a) (b)

   (c) (d)

2. (a) (b)

   (c) (d)

3. (a) (b)

   (c) (d)

4. (a) April   (b) February
   (c) November   (d) September

5. (a) (b)

   (c) (d)

6. (a) January   (b) December
   (c) June   (d) August

7. (a) A   (b) O
   (c) U   (d) T

8. (a) F   (b) B
   (c) U   (d) V

9. (a) 37   (b) 47
   (c) 57   (d) 66

10. (a) AB   (b) CD
    (c) EF   (d) MH

11. (a) ABC   (b) DEF
    (c) GHI   (d) ZXY

12.
    (a)   (b)   (c)   (d)

13.
    (a)   (b)   (c)   (d)

14. (a) (b)

    (c) (d)

15.
    (a)   (b)   (c)   (d)

16.
    (a)   (b)   (c)   (d)

17.
    (a)   (b)   (c)   (d)

18.
    (a)   (b)   (c)   (d)

19.

(a) (b) (c) (d)

20.

(a) (b) (c) (d)

Measuring Units

4

CHAPTER SUMMARY

Length

It includes comparison of the lengths of the objects by measuring the length of the given objects with the help of ruler. For the curved objects, count the curves. Curves having maximum number of curves is longest and curve with minimum number of curves is the shortest.

Weights

Compare the weights by using weighing scale.

Money:

$$1 \text{ Rupee } = 100 \text{ paise}$$

$$\text{so, } 1 \text{ Paisa} = \frac{1}{100} \text{ rupee}$$

Time:

1 hour = 60 minutes
1 minute = 60 seconds
Number of days in a week = 7
Number of months in a year = 12

Example:

Which is the lightest shape?

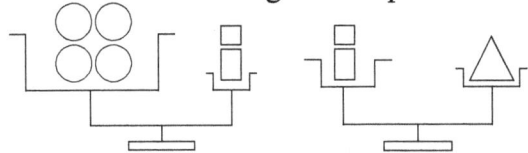

(A) ◯

(B) ▢

(C) △

(D) None of these

Answer: A

Explanation: ▢ = ◯◯ and △ = ▢▢

So ◯ is the lightest shape.

MULTIPLE CHOICE QUESTIONS

1. Which fruit is the heaviest?

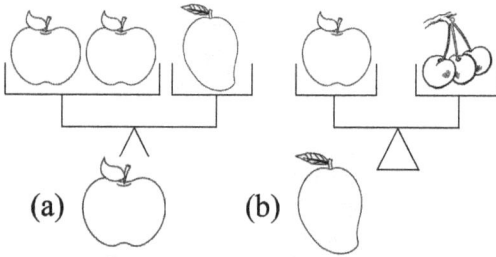

   (a)

   (b)

   (c)

   (d) Can't be determined

2. Which string is shortest?

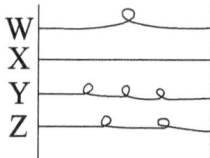

   (a) X   (b) W

   (c) Z   (d) Y

3. Which tube has maximum capacity?

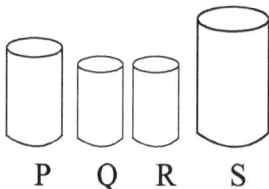

   P   Q   R   S

   (a) Q   (b) R

   (c) P   (d) S

4. How much is the total given money?

   (a) 160   (b) 167

   (c) 150   (d) 175

5. Which is the longest pen?

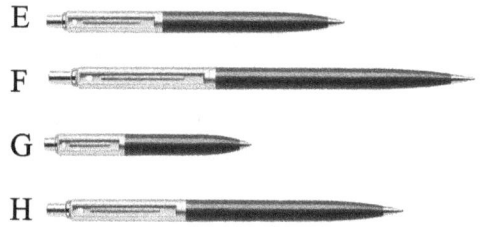

   (a) G   (b) E

   (c) F   (d) H

6.

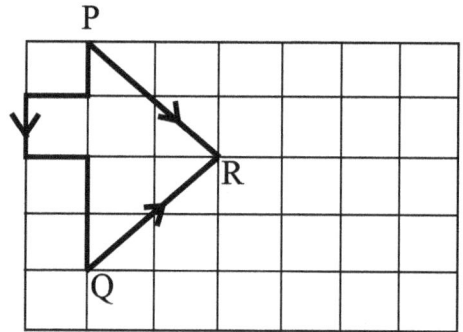

   Naina walks along PQ, Sneha walks along QR and Saina walks along PR. Which statement is correct?

   (a) Naina and Saina have covered the same distance.

   (b) Sneha has covered maximum distance.

   (c) Both Sneha and Saina have covered same distance.

   (d) All are incorrect.

7. Which clock show the time " two and a half hour after 2:45 P.M.?

   P   Q   R   S

(a) P   (b) R

(c) Q   (d) S

8. Which toy costs the least?

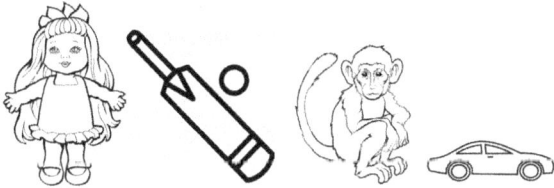

₹400   ₹590   ₹375   ₹859

(a) Car   (b) Bat

(c) Monkey   (d) Doll

9. How many seconds are there in 2 hours?

(a) 7200   (b) 720

(c) 3600   (d) 360

10. Count the money.

₹1   ₹10   ₹2   ₹5   ₹10

₹1   ₹2   ₹1   ₹5   ₹1   ₹2

(a) ₹42   (b) ₹45

(c) ₹40   (d) ₹32

11. How many ways I can reach to point S from point P?

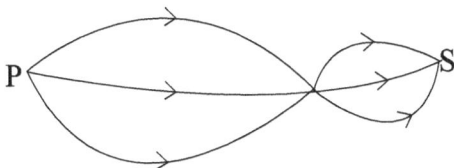

(a) 7   (b) 9

(c) 12   (d) 10

12. Aman starts his cricket practice on 10th May 20xx. He finishes his practice on 24th May 20xx. On which day he finished his practice? (Assume Aman practices on Sunday also).

May 20xx						
S	M	T	W	T	F	S
		1	2	3	4	5
6	7	8	9	10	11	12
13	14	15	16	17	18	19
20	21	22	23	24	25	26
27	28	29	30	31		

(a) Tuesday   (b) Monday

(c) Thursday   (d) Friday

13. If today is Saturday, then day before yesterday _____.

(a) Sunday   (b) Thursday

(c) Monday   (d) Tuesday

14. If Monday falls on 6 January then next Monday falls on _____ January.

(a) 11   (b) 12

(c) 13   (d) 10

15. Arrange the given animals from the heaviest to lightest.

P   Q   R

(a) Q,P,R   (b) P,R,Q,

(c) R,P,Q   (d) Q,R,P

16. How many 15 minutes are there in 1 hour?

(a) 2   (b) 3

(c) 4   (d) 5

17.

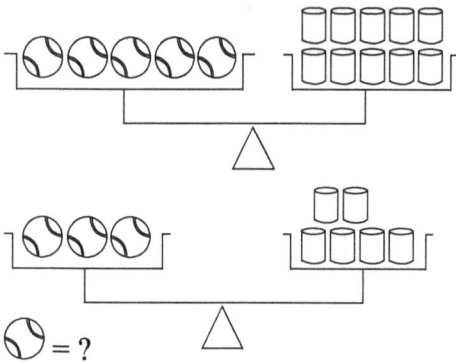

= ?

(a) ⬚⬚   (b) ⬚

(c) ⬚⬚⬚   (d) ⬚⬚⬚⬚

18. Where will be minute hand of a clock when the clock shows quarter to 8?

    (a) 10   (b) 9

    (c) 6   (d) 3

19. If Box X is heavier than Box Y, but lighter than Box Z. Which of the following is correct?

(a) X   Y   (b) Y   X

(c) Z   X   (d) Cann't determined

20. If 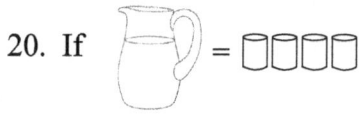 = ⬚⬚⬚⬚

Then _____ ⬚ will fill up 6 such jugs.

    (a) 18   (b) 24

    (c) 12   (d) 20

Geometrical Shapes

Learning Objectives : In this chapter, students will learn about:
- ✓ Recognizing Geometrical Shapes

CHAPTER SUMMARY

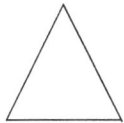 Rectangle		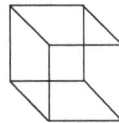 Cube	
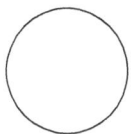 Square		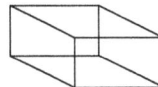 Cuboids	
Triangle		 Slanting lines	
Circle		Vertical lines	
 Cone		Horizontal lines/ Sleeping lines	
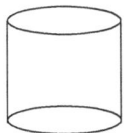 Cylinder		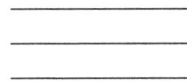 Curved lines	

1. The below given figure is made up of _____ circles.

    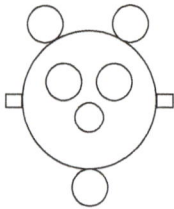

    (a) 6   (b) 7
    (c) 8   (d) 10

2. Count the number of squares and triangles.

    (a) 3, 6   (b) 3, 5
    (c) 2, 5   (d) 2, 6

3. Count the straight lines.

    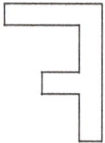

    (a) 9   (b) 10
    (c) 11   (d) 12

4. The below given figure has _____ triangles.

    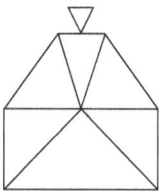

    (a) 9   (b) 8
    (c) 7   (d) 10

5. The below given figure has _____ squares.

    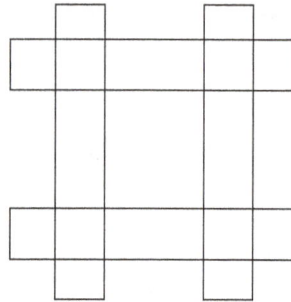

    (a) 12   (b) 11
    (c) 10   (d) 8

6. How many sleeping lines are there in the given figure.

    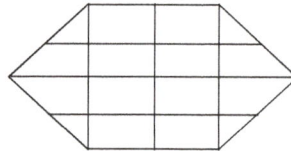

    (a) 4   (b) 5
    (c) 3   (d) 0

7. The given figure has ____ horizontal lines _____ vertical lines and slant _____ lines.

    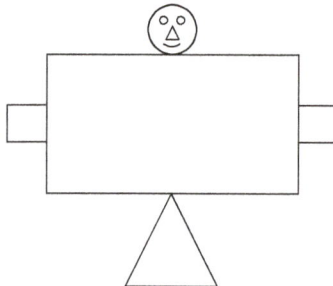

    (a) 8, 4, 5   (b) 8, 3, 4
    (c) 8, 4, 4   (d) 7, 4, 4

8. There are _____ more triangles than the squares in the below given figure.

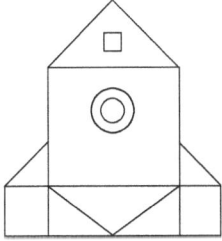

   (a) 3   (b) 4
   (c) 2   (d) 1

9. Count the number of slanting lines.

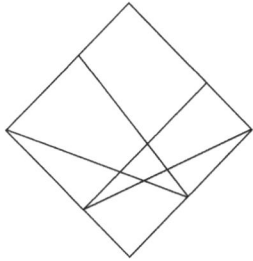

   (a) 5   (b) 7
   (c) 9   (d) 8

10. Count the number of straight lines.

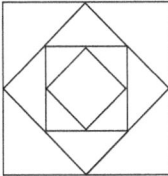

   (a) 12   (b) 16
   (c) 10   (d) 18

11. How many triangle are used to make this pattern?

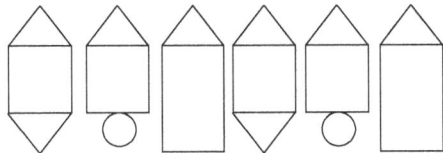

   (a) 6   (b) 8
   (c) 10   (d) 12

12. How many curved lines are there in the figure?

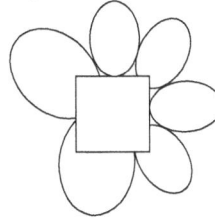

   (a) 7   (b) 4
   (c) 6   (d) 5

13. The given figure has _____ circles, _____ straight lines and _____ triangles.

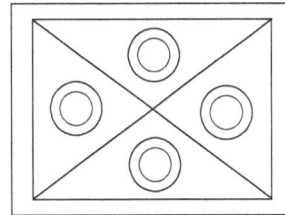

   (a) 8, 10, 8   (b) 8, 10, 6
   (c) 7, 5, 3   (d) 4, 5, 8

14. The given figure has _____ curves

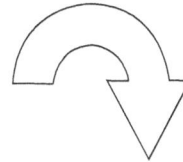

   (a) 2   (b) 3
   (c) 4   (d) 0

15. Identify the shape of the shaded face of the given solid.

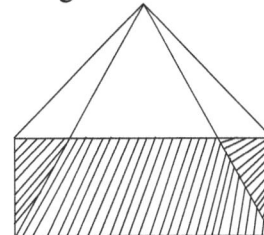

   (a) Square   (b) Rectangle
   (c) Triangle   (d) Circle

16. How many curves are there in the figure?

(a) 6   (b) 3
(c) 5   (d) 4

17. Given figure is made up of _____ triangles, _____ circles, _____ square and _____ rectangles.

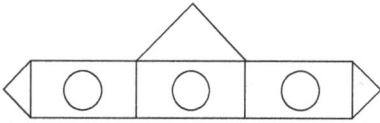

(a) 3, 3, 0, 2   (b) 3, 2, 1, 2
(c) 3, 1, 3, 2   (d) 2, 2, 1, 3

18. Given figure has _____ circles and _____ triangles.

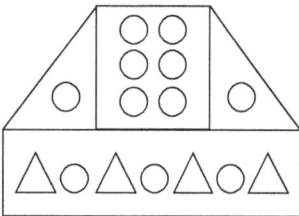

(a) 10, 6   (b) 11, 4
(c) 11, 6   (d) 10, 4

19. Which shape is not present in the given box?

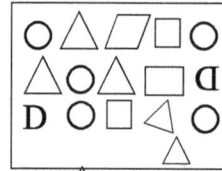

(a) △   (b) ○
(c) ⌂   (d) □

20. How many feat faces are there in the given figure?

(a) 5   (b) 2
(c) 1   (d) None of these

Ranking Test

Learning Objectives : In this chapter, students will learn about:
- ✓ Basics of Ranking

CHAPTER SUMMARY

In this chapter, relative positions or ranking of different groups of persons or objects is given.

You are required to establish the ranking or position of other individuals in the same group with respect to one another.

There are two types of questions:

(i) Based on order

(ii) Based on ranking

Example : Observe the given figures carefully and answer the following question.

Left/first

P Q R S T U V W

_____ ball is fourth from the right end:

(a) S   (b) T

(c) R   (d) P

Answer (b)

Explanation : Ball W is first from the right. So, Ball T is fourth from the right end.

MULTIPLE CHOICE QUESTIONS

Direction : (1–6) Observe the given figure and answer the following questions.

(Left)  (Right)

1. Which flag is 2nd from the right end?
   (a) Q   (b) V
   (c) S   (d) W

2. _____ is fourth from right end?
   (a) S   (b) U
   (c) P   (d) T

3. Which flag is between flag R and Flag T?
   (a) P   (b) U
   (c) S   (d) W

4. Which flag is fourth from right and fifth from left end?
   (a) P   (b) W
   (c) T   (d) S

5. If we make one more flag in row after Flag W, then which flag is in the middle of row?
   (a) P   (b) Q
   (c) R   (d) T

6. Flag _____ is in right of flag U is and in left of Flag W.
   (a) S   (b) T
   (c) V   (d) P

Direction (7–11) : Observe the given figures carefully and answer the following questions.

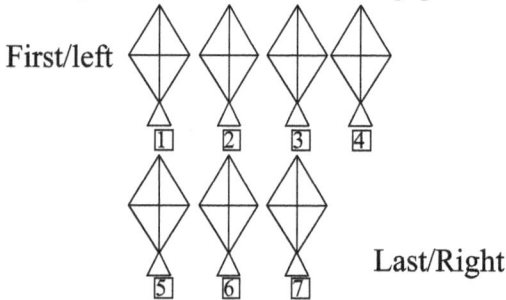

First/left

Last/Right

7. Which kite is in the middle of row?
   (a) 1   (b) 3
   (c) 4   (d) 7

8. Which kite is 3rd from right end and 5th from left end?
   (a) 2   (b) 7
   (c) 4   (d) 5

9. Which kite is in immediate left of Kite 6?
   (a) 5   (b) 3
   (c) 7   (d) 1

10. Kite_____ is second to left of Kite 5?
    (a) 7   (b) 5
    (c) 3   (d) 4

11. Kite 6 is fourth to right of kite _____
    (a) 7   (b) 2
    (c) 1   (d) 7

Direction (12–15) : Observe the given figures carefully and answer the following questions.

First/left

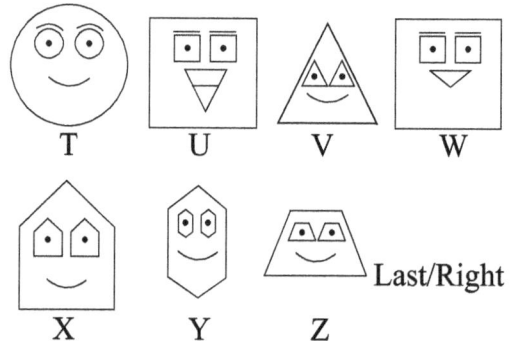

Last/Right

12. Shape _____ is in immediate left of figure X and in immediate right of figure V.
    (a) W   (b) Y
    (c) U   (d) T

13. If shape T and W are removed from above series, then shape _____ is in middle of the series.
    (a) T   (b) Z
    (c) X   (d) U

14. Shape _____ is sixth from left end.
    (a) U   (b) Z
    (c) V   (d) Y

15. Shape _____ is second to right of shape W.
    (a) U   (b) Y
    (c) Z   (d) T

Direction (16–17): observe the given word and answer the following questions.

    B E A U T I F U L

16. Which is third vowel from the right end?
    (a) I   (b) A
    (c) E   (d) U

17. If B, I and F are removed, then _____ is third to the left to L.
    (a) T   (b) E
    (c) U   (d) A

18. There are three rivers — Ganga, Yamuna and Narmada.
    (i)   Yamuna is larger than Narmada
    (ii) Ganga is larger than Narmada but smaller than Yamuna
    (iii) Which is the largest river?
        (a) Yamuna
        (b) Ganga
        (c) Narmada
        (d) Can't Determined

19.
    P Q R S T U V
    If Pencil P and S interchange their positions, then which pencil will be fourth to the left of Pencil T?
    (a) Q   (b) V
    (c) P   (d) S

20. Which of the following is fifth to the right of second item from the left?

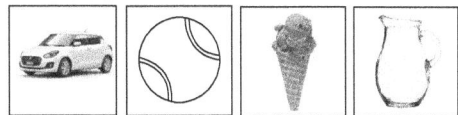

    (a)   (b)   (c)   (d)

Grouping of Figures and Embedded Figures

Learning Objectives : In this chapter, students will learn about:
- ✓ Embedded Figures

CHAPTER SUMMARY

Grouping of Figures

In this type of questions, you are required to analyze the given set of pictures or numbers to classify them into groups.

Embedded Figures

A figure (X) is said to be embedded in a figure (Y) if Figure (Y) contains Figure (X) as its part.

Example : How many groups of 2's can be formed ?

(a) 7   (b) 6

(c) 8   (d) 9

Answer (b)

Explanation :

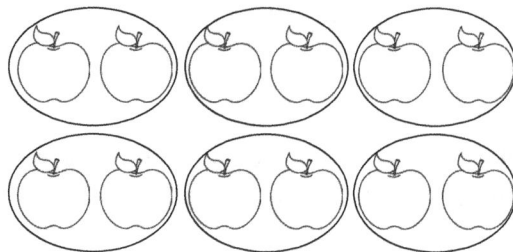

There are 6 groups.

MULTIPLE CHOICE QUESTIONS

Direction (1 – 7): Which of the following part is exactly embedded in the given figure without any orientation?

1.

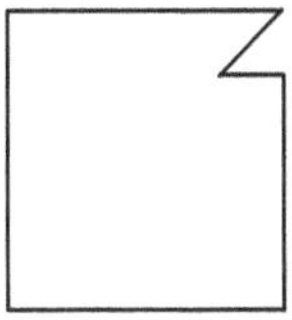

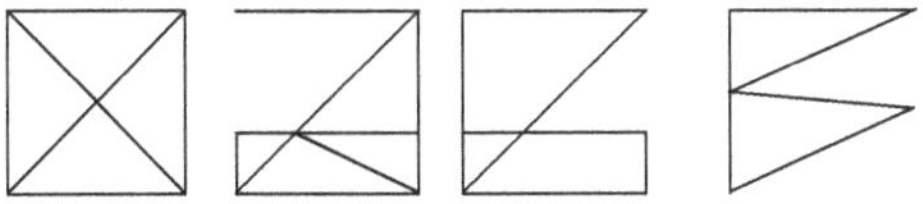

(a) (b) (c) (d)

2.

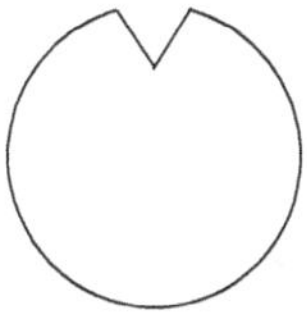

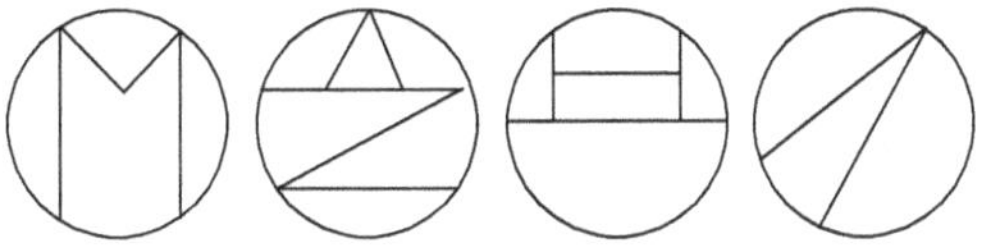

(a) (b) (c) (d)

3.

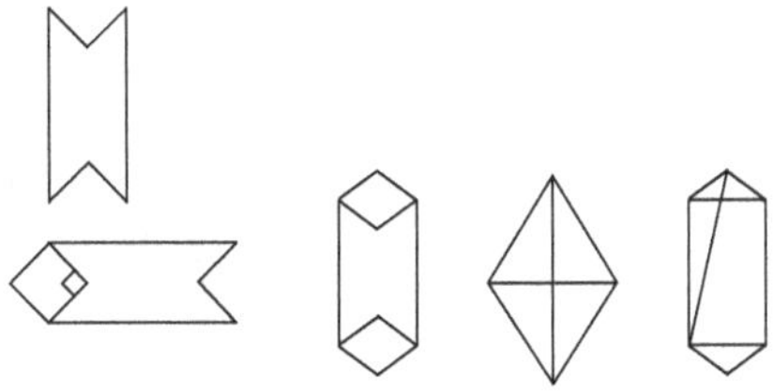

(a) (b) (c) (d)

4.

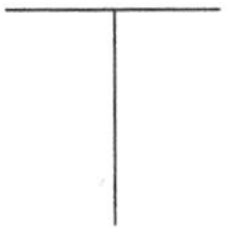

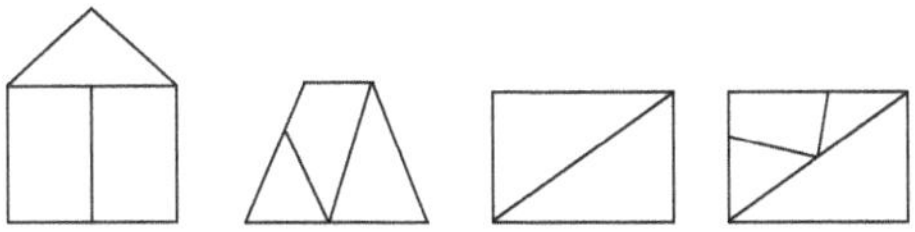

(a) (b) (c) (d)

5.

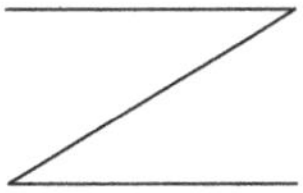

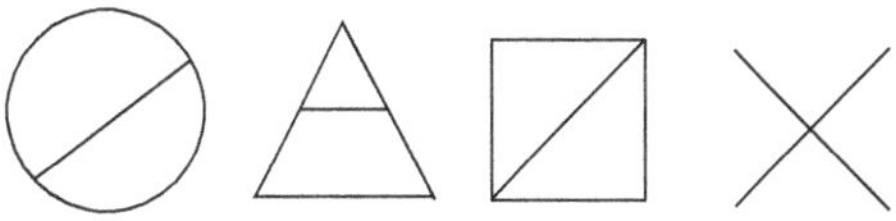

(a) (b) (c) (d)

6.

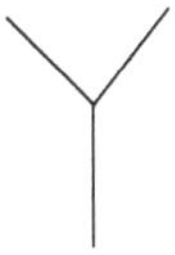

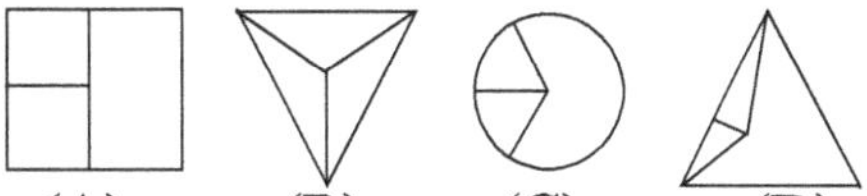

(A) (B) (C) (D)

7.

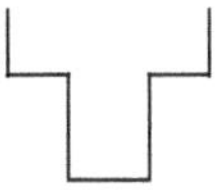

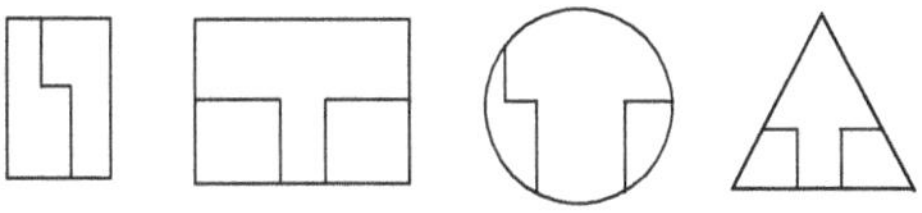

(a) (b) (c) (d)

8. How many grougs of 4 balls (if there are 5 balls in each box) can be formed from these balls?

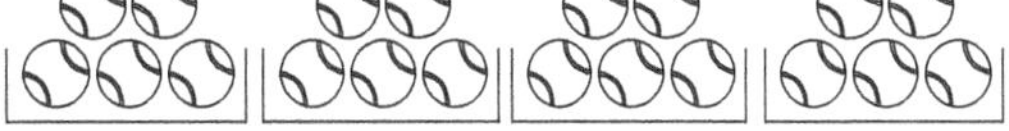

(a) 6 (b) 5
(c) 3 (d) 6

9. How many grougs of 3 pencils can be formed from the given pencils.?

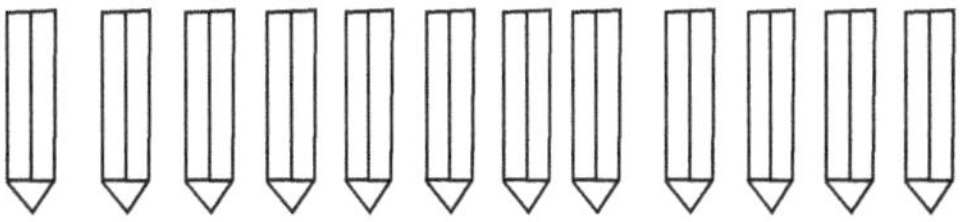

(a) 5   (b) 6

(c) 4   (d) 7

10. How many groups of 4 stars can be formed from given stars?

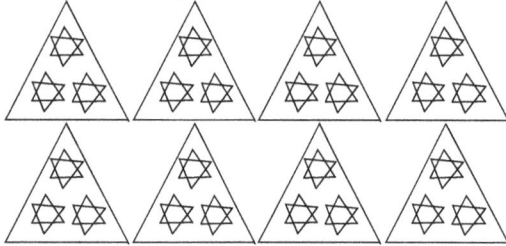

(a) 5   (b) 6

(c) 7   (d) 8

11. Identify the group of 4 eights from the given options.

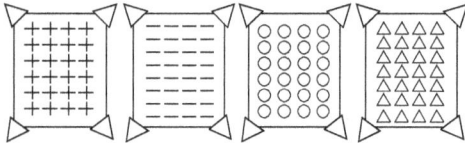

(a)   (b)   (c)   (d)

12. Identify the group of 5 sevens.

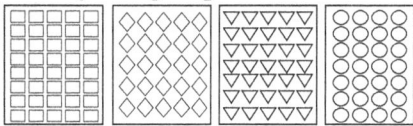

(a)   (b)   (c)   (d)

13. Number 13 belongs to _____.

GROUP W	GROUP X	GROUP Y	GROUP Z
1 5 9	2 4 6 8	5 15 25	7 12 17
13 17 21	10 12 14 16	35 45 55	22 27 32
25 29 33	18 20 22 24	65 75 85	37 42 47

(a) Group X   (b) Group W

(c) Group Y   (d) Group Z

14. The shape given below belongs to group _____.

Group M   Group N   Group O   Group P

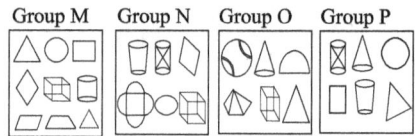

(a) M   (b) O

(c) N   (d) P

15. How many groups of 2 squares can be formed from given shapes?

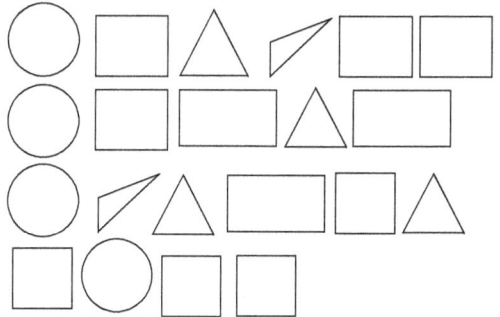

(a) 5   (b) 4

(c) 3   (d) 2

16. Shubham purchased 12 toffees from market.

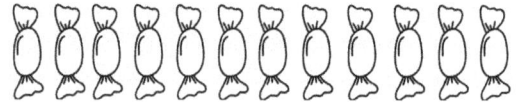

How many toffees are there in each group if 3 groups having same number of toffees are formed?

(a) 4   (c) 15

(c) 18   (d) 20

17. John has stickers of different expressions. He decides to classify the stickers on the basis of expressions. Then he classified in this way.

Find the option which relates the given classification.

(a) 4 groups of 3

(b) 5 groups of 4

(c) 3 groups of 4

(d) 3 Groups of 5

18. Which combination of letters is hidden in the given logo?

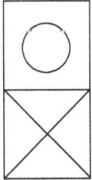

(a) DAQ   (b) GPY

(c) OXE   (d) MQP

19. Which of the following words is hidden in the given image?

(a) RAT   (b) MAT

(c) BAT   (d) CUP

20. Select a figure from the options in which figure (x) is exactly embedded as one of its part.

Figure (X)

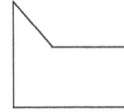

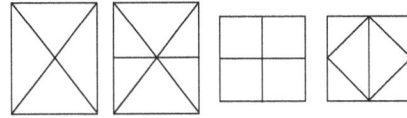

(a)   (b)   (c)   (d)

Coding-Decoding

Learning Objectives : In this chapter, students will learn about:
- ✓ Coding and Decoding

CHAPTER SUMMARY

In this type of test, some particular words are given certain substituted names. After this a question is asked, that needs to be answered in the same substituted code language.

Example : If 'Pen' is called 'Wood', 'Wood' is called Fan, Fan is called Chairs, Chair is called Wall, then on which of following will a person sit?

(a) Fan   (b) Wood

(c) Chair   (d) Wall

Explanation : 'Chair' is called wall.

1. If 'Potato' is called 'Tomato'. 'Tomato' is called 'Radish', 'Radish' is called 'Onion', then the colour of which vegetable is Red.

   (a) Potato   (b) Radish

   (c) Tomato   (d) Onion

2. If 'Sky' is called 'Sea', 'Sea' is called 'Water' 'Water' is called 'Air'. 'Air' is called 'Cloud', then what do we drink when thirsty?

   (a) Sky   (b) Water

   (c) Air   (d) Cloud

3. If 'Circle' is called 'Square' 'Square' is called 'Triangle'. 'Triangle' is called 'Line segment', then which shape has four sides?

   (a) Circle   (b) Square

   (c) Triangle   (d) None of these

4. If 'Tiger' is called 'Cow', 'Cow' is called 'Butterfly' then who eats flesh?

   (a) Tiger   (b) Cow

   (c) Butterfly   (d) None of these

5. If 'Water' is called 'Blue', 'Blue' is called 'Red', 'Red' is called 'White', 'White' is called 'Sky' then which of following is the colour of milk?

   (a) Blue   (b) Red

   (c) White   (d) Sky

6. If 'Rhino' is called 'Elephant', 'Elephant' is called 'Tiger', 'Tiger' is called 'Cow', then national animal of India is _____.

   (a) Rhino   (b) Elephant

   (c) Cow   (d) Tiger

7. If 'Morning' is called 'Noon', 'Noon' is called 'Evening', Evening is called 'Night' then when do we do breakfast?

   (a) Noon   (b) Morning

   (c) Evening   (d) Night

8. If 'Cycle' is called 'Auto-rickshaw, 'Auto-rickshaw' is called 'Car', 'Car' is called 'Truck' then which of the following is three-wheeler?

   (a) Car   (b) Truck

   (c) Cycle   (d) None of these

9. If 'Soap' is called 'Honey', Honey is called 'Butter', 'Butter' is called Oil, then what do we eat with bread?

   (a) Butter   (b) Honey

   (c) Oil   (d) Soap

10. If 'Pen' is called 'Wood', 'Wood' is called 'Chair', 'Chair', is called Grass, then _____ is used for writing.

    (a) Pen   (b) Wood

    (c) Grass   (d) Chair

11. If 'Sky' is called 'Water', 'Water' is called 'Air', 'Air' is called 'Tree' then where does fish live?

    (a) Sky   (b) Water

    (c) Tree   (d) Air

12. If '5' is called '10', '10' is called '21', '21' is called '50', then what is the sum of 15 and 6?

    (a) 5   (b) 50

    (c) 21   (d) 10

13. If 'X' called '÷', '÷' is called '+', '+' is called '−' then which symbol is used for addition?

    (a) −   (b) +

    (c) X   (d) '÷'

14. If 'Leg' is called 'Hand', 'Hand' is called 'Teeth', 'Teeth' is called 'Ear', then which body part is used to chew anything?

    (a) Leg   (b) Teeth

    (c) Ear   (d) Hand

15. If ○ is called '◡', '◡' is called '✡', '✡' is called 🜨, then which gives us light?

    (a)   (b)

    (c)   (d)

16. If ◌ is called ◌, ◌ is called ◡, ◡is called ◌, then which of these is of red colour?

    (a)   (b)

    (c)   (d)

17. If ▢ is called ◡, ◡ is called ✎, ✎ is called ◯, ◯ is called ◜ then which of the following is used to cook food?

    (a)   (b)

    (c)   (d)

18. If ✏ is called ✎, ✎ is called 🍶, 🍶 is called ▭, ▭ is called ⊡ then which of the following is used to drink water?

    (a)   (b)

    (c)   (d)

19. If ✿ is called ⌐, ⌐ is called 👂, 👂 is called 🦵, 🦵 then which body part is used to see things?

    (a)   (b)

    (c)   (d)

20. If 'Monday', is called 'Thursday', 'Thursday, is called 'Friday', 'Friday' is called 'Tuesday',, Tuesday' is called 'Sunday' then what day comes after Thursday?

    (a) Monday   (b) Thursday

    (c) Tuesday   (d) Friday

SECTION 3
ACHIEVERS' SECTION

Thoughtful Questions

Some Important Concepts

Multiplication and Division

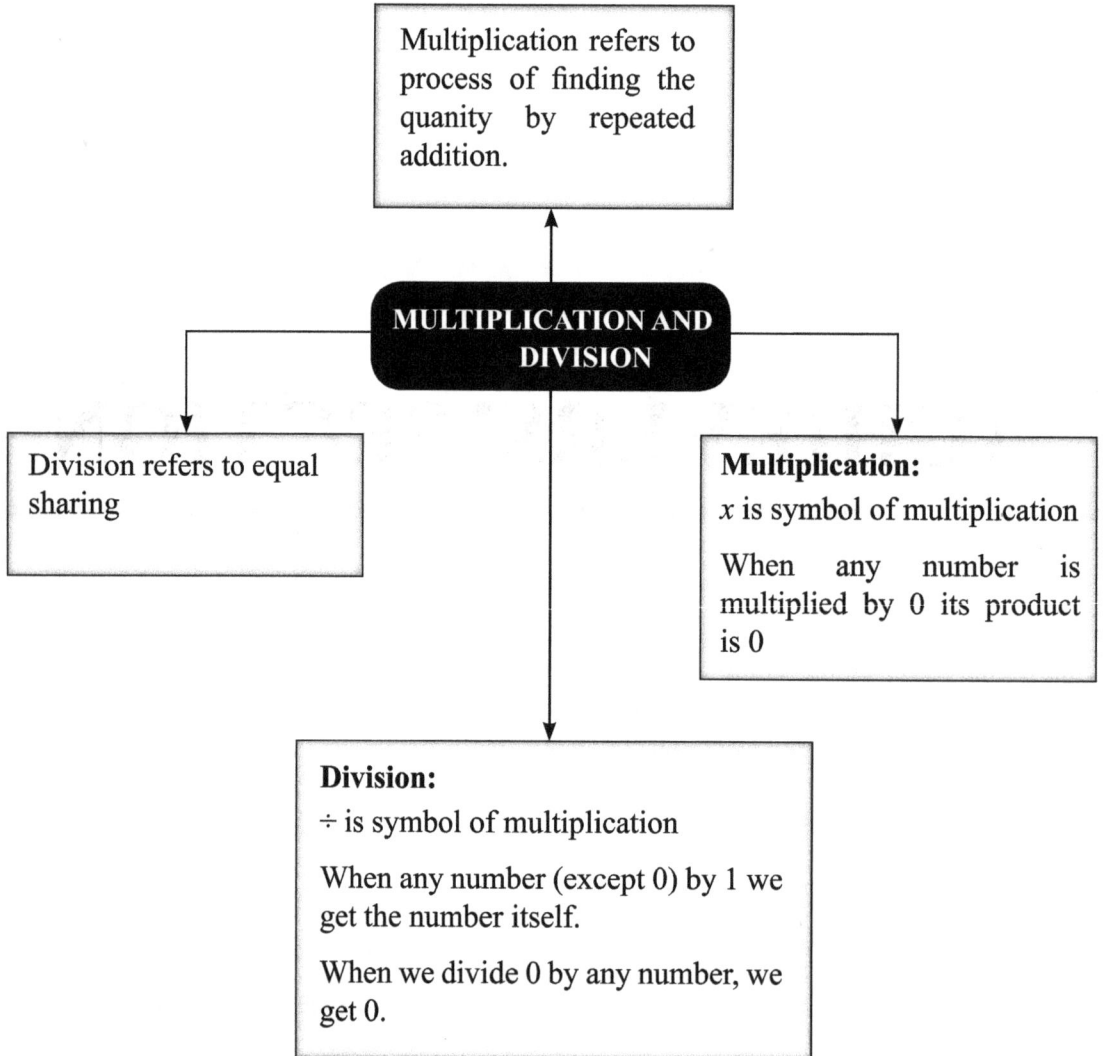

Multiplication refers to process of finding the quanity by repeated addition.

MULTIPLICATION AND DIVISION

Division refers to equal sharing

Multiplication:

x is symbol of multiplication

When any number is multiplied by 0 its product is 0

Division:

÷ is symbol of multiplication

When any number (except 0) by 1 we get the number itself.

When we divide 0 by any number, we get 0.

Shape

```
                    ┌─────────────────────────┐
                    │ Three Dimensional - 3D:  │
                    │ Sphere, Cylinder, Cube,  │
                    │ Cuboid and Cone          │
                    └─────────────────────────┘
                                ▲
                                │
                    ┌──────────────────┐
                    │     SHAPES        │
                    └──────────────────┘
              ┌──────────┴──────────┐
              ▼                     ▼
┌─────────────────────────┐   ┌─────────────────────────────┐
│ Lines: Straight line     │   │ Two dimensional - 2D:        │
│ (Horizontal,  Vertical   │   │ Circle,  rectangle,  square, │
│ lines) and curved line   │   │ oval, triangle               │
└─────────────────────────┘   └─────────────────────────────┘
```

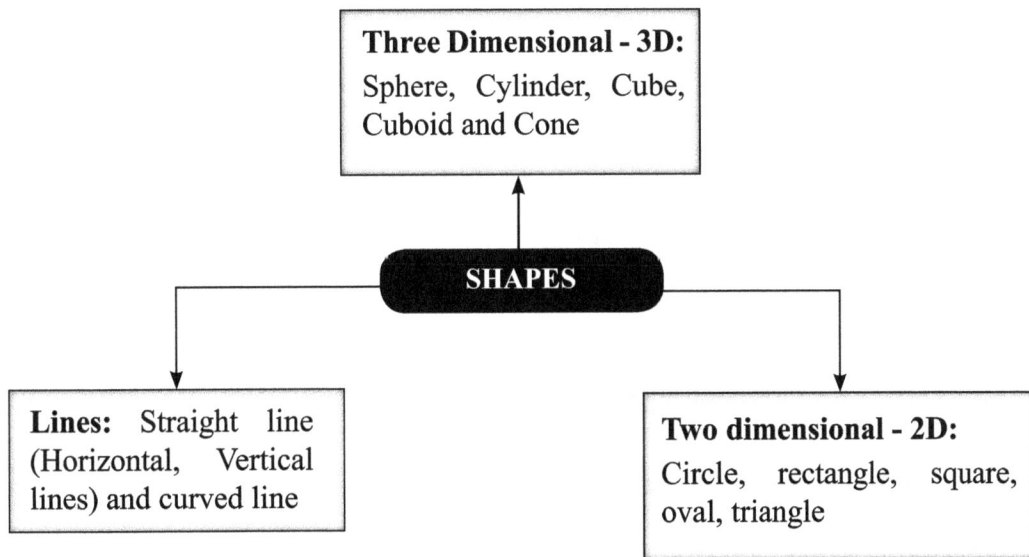

Some thoughtful questions

1. **Look at the picture and write**

(a) How many are pulling the carrot out?
    Answer: 6
(b) Who was the first one to pull it?
    Answer: Old man
(c) The cat is _____ in the line.
    Answer: Fifth
(d) Who was the fourth one to pull the carrot? _____
    Answer: The dog
(e) How many were pulling the carrot before the cat came to help them?
    Answer: 4

2. **Draw a line to match the heavier one.**

(a)

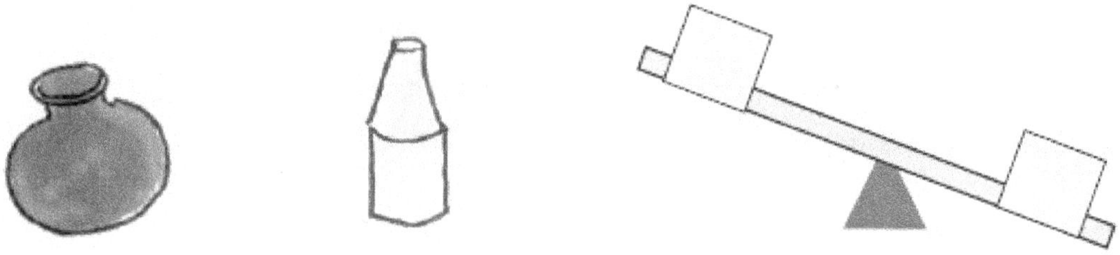

(b)

(c)

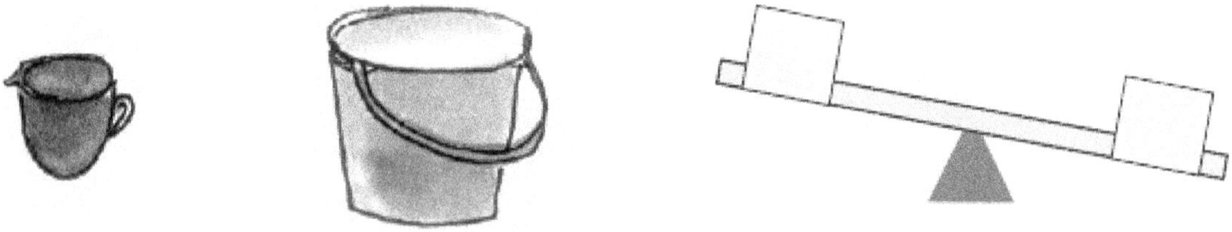

Answer:

(a)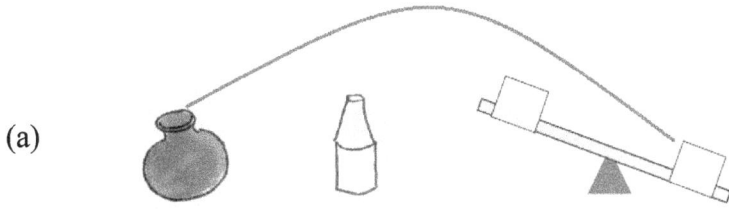

(b)

(c)

3. **Some children of Class II–A love to play "Teacher – Teacher". They have decided to take turns in playing the teacher's role.**

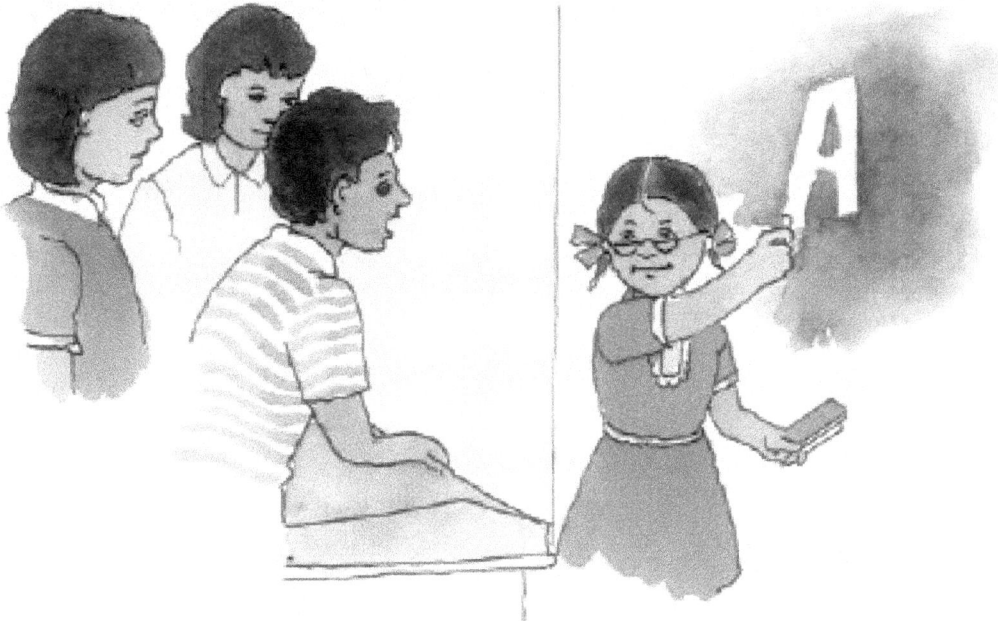

Day	Who will play teacher role
Monday	Nagesh
Tuesday	Pinki
Wednesday	Ankit
Thursday	Sheetal
Friday	Navneet
Saturday	Golu

Now fill in the blanks:

(a) _____ will be the teacher the day after Friday.

Answer:

Golu will be the teacher the day after Friday.

(b) _____ will play the teacher's role on the day before Tuesday.

Answer:

Nagesh will play the teacher's role on the day before Tuesday.

(c) Ankit will play the teacher's role on the day after _____.

Answer:

Ankit will play the teacher's role on the day after Tuesday.

(d) Navneet will play the teacher's role on the day before _____.

Answer:

Navneet will play the teacher's role on the day before Saturday.

Section I : Logical Reasoning

1. Find the missing shape.

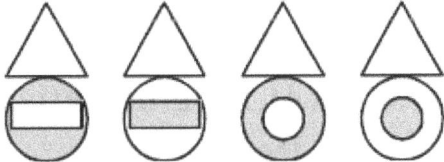

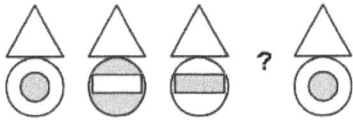

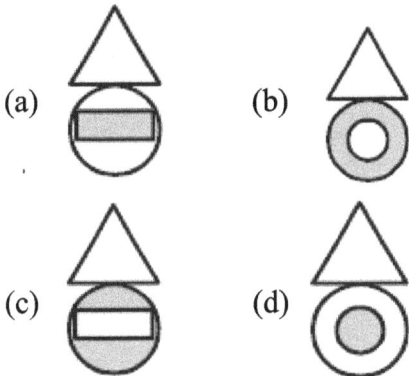

(a)

(b)

(c)

(d)

2. If Meeku jumps like this then what will be the next number on his stone?

(a) 29   (b) 28

(c) 31   (d) 27

3. How long did Golu take to complete his homework?

Started doing homework   Completed homework

(a) 2 hours 20 minutes

(b) 2 hours

(c) 1 hour 40 minutes

(d) 1 hour 20 minutes

4. Look at the two balance scales given below :

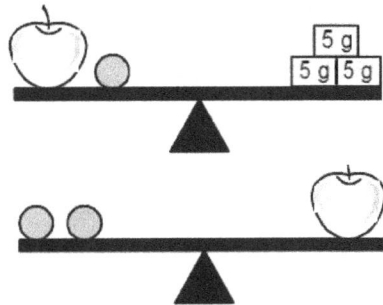

The mass of each ⬡ is _____ g.

(a) 3   (b) 10

(c) 5   (d) 15

5. Look at the Ashu's picture and tell how many different circles are there?

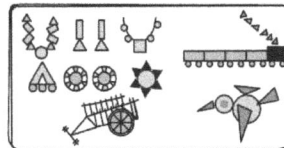

(a) 24   (b) 26

(c) 28   (d) 30

6. What is the length (in cm) of the pen?

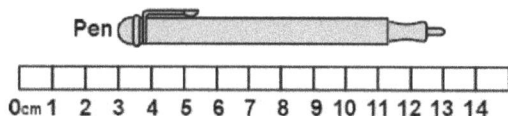

(a) 13 cm   (b) 12 cm
(c) 10 cm   (d) 9 cm

7. Find the missing number.

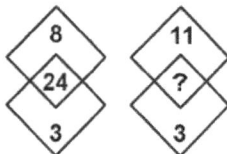

(a) 12   (b) 3
(c) 28   (d) 33

8. The Hamburger is _____ g heavier than the hot dog.

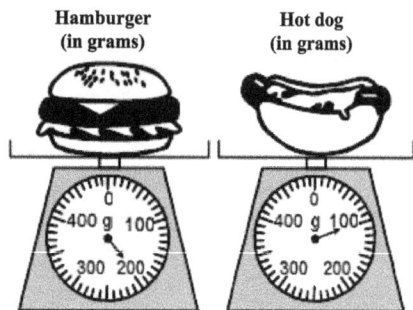

(a) 100   (b) 120
(c) 140   (d) 80

9. Which box is the lightest?

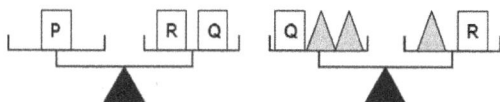

(a) P
(b) Q
(c) R
(d) Can't be determined

10. How many rectangles can you find in the figure.

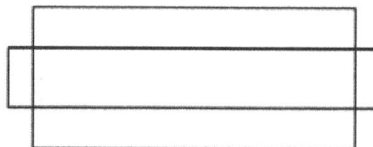

(a) 8   (b) 9
(c) 11   (d) 10

Section II : Mathematical Reasoning

11. Shraddha made some shapes in her picture. How many sleeping lines are there?

(a) 1   (b) 10
(c) 3   (d) 4

12. Which is the next figure in the given pattern?

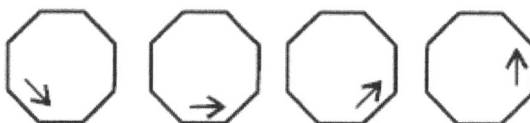

(a)   (b)

(c)   (d)

13. What is the number represented by each

     ?

    | 30 | 48 | 18 |

    (a) 6   (b) 8
    (c) 10   (d) 16

14. What is the missing number in the given pattern?

    5A, 6B, 7C, ... 9E

    (a) 8D   (b) 8C
    (c) 10E   (d) 9D

15. I have 2 circular faces. I have a curved face. Soft drink cans often look like me. Who am I?

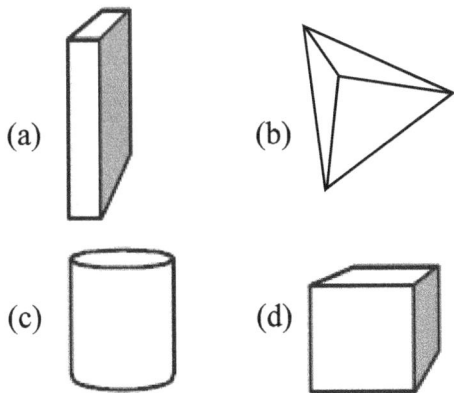

16. Which figure does not belong with the other three?

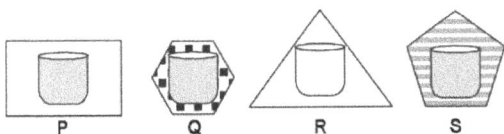

17. What will be the 11th shape in the pattern given below?

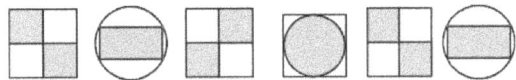

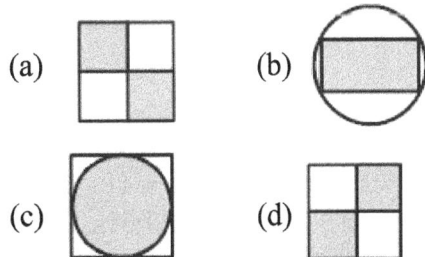

    (a)   (b)

    (c)   (d)

18. A papaya tree is 2 m shorter than the tree shown here. The total height of the papaya tree and the tree shown is _____ m.

    (a) 2 m   (b) 3 m
    (c) 5 m   (d) 8 m

19. What is the difference of greatest and smallest number?

    (a) 24   (b) 3
    (c) 32   (d) 14

(a) P   (b) Q
(c) R   (d) S

20. What fraction of the figure is shaded?

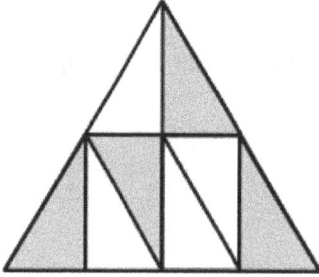

(a) 2/3 (b) 3/8
(c) 4/12 (d) 4/8

21. Mr. Mehra had 25 stamps. He shared the stamps equally among 5 boys. Each boy received _____ stamps.
(a) 5 (b) 10
(c) 32 (d) 23

22. Which of the following containers contain most amount of water?

Container A   Container B   Container C   Container D

(a) Container A (b) Container B
(c) Container C (d) Container D

23. Shraddha opened 4 new bottles of grape juice and poured the juice into glasses as shown below:

Bottle II contains 2 more glasses of grape juice than _____
(a) Bottle I (b) Bottle II
(c) Bottle IV (d) None of these

24. The adjoining picture graph shows the number of each type of pet in Golu's pet shop. How many more fishes than cats does Golu's shop have?

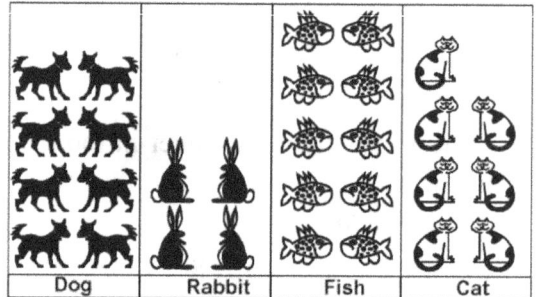

| Dog | Rabbit | Fish | Cat |

(a) 7 (b) 10
(c) 3 (d) 8

25. How many groups of 10 can these toy cars form?

(a) 12 (b) 2
(c) 8 (d) 6

Section III : Everyday Mathematics

26. How many months has 31 days?
(a) 4 (b) 8
(c) 7 (d) 6

27. Lisa saw 3 spiders in a garden. How many legs did she see in all?

(a) 12   (b) 24

(c) 48   (d) 36

28. I am a number between $25 \div 5$ and $21 \div 3$. What number am I?

(a) 5   (b) 7

(c) 6   (d) 9

29. $10 \times$ _____ $= 5 + 5 + 5 + 5 + 5 + 5 + 5 + 5 + 5$

(a) 10   (b) 5

(c) 0   (d) 2

30. Golu made the adjoining picture graph. What is the total number of boys who play badminton and football?

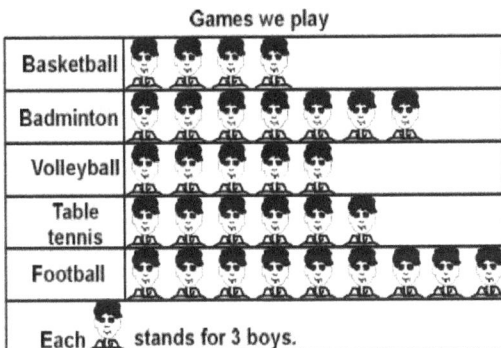

Games we play

Basketball	
Badminton	
Volleyball	
Table tennis	
Football	

Each 👦 stands for 3 boys.

(a) 12   (b) 24

(c) 16   (d) 48

Section IV : Achievers' Section

31. How many of these letters have both curves and straight lines?

A B C D E F G

(a) 3   (b) 2

(c) 4   (d) 6

32. I am a 2-digit number. My one's digit is 4 times my ten's digit. My ten's digit is 2. What am I?

(a) 24   (b) 28

(c) 22   (d) 42

33. The cost of each item is given below: If Jiah spent ₹ 348, what were the two items she bought?

Handbag   Dress   Shoes   Necklace

₹ 95   ₹ 253   ₹ 108   ₹ 464

(a) The handbag and pair of shoes

(b) The handbag and the dress

(c) The dress and the pair of shoes

(d) The pair of shoes and the necklace

34. A kettle of water can fill upto 3 teaspots. A teapot of water can fill up 4 cups. A kettle can fill up _____ cups.

(a) 3   (b) 8

(c) 4   (d) 12

35. Dia walks 512 m to get to the supermarket from her house. She has to walk another 128 m to get to the church. Aryan's house is 120 m farther from the church than Dia's house. How far is Aryan's house from the church?

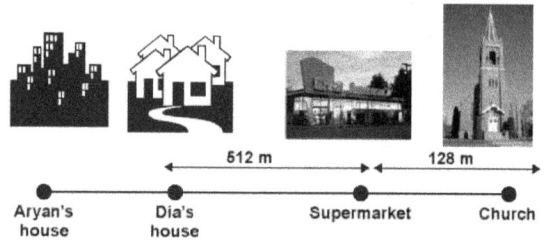

512 m   128 m

Aryan's house   Dia's house   Supermarket   Church

(a) 192 m   (b) 760 m

(c) 640 m   (d) 248 m

Model Test Paper

Section I : Logical Reasoning

1. If L means minus, A means 5, B means 3, then A L B = ?
   (a) 2
   (b) 5
   (c) 0
   (d) None of these

2. In which direction X has to move to reach the given position?

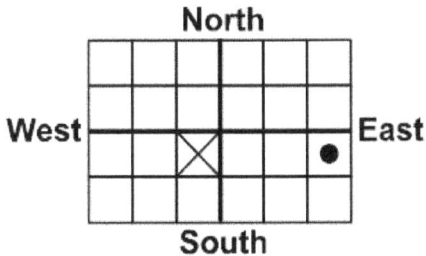

   (a) East
   (b) West
   (c) North
   (d) South

3. Which day comes after Tuesday?
   (a) Monday
   (b) Sunday
   (c) Wednesday
   (d) Friday

4. Shraddha had four ₹ 5 coins. She exchanged her money with some notes. If she got 2 notes, which figure shows the amount she got?

   (a)

   (b)

   (c)

   (d)

5. Shubhra has fifty ₹ 2 coins. If she puts them one over the other which geometrical figure will she get?

   (a)
   (b)

   (c)
   (d)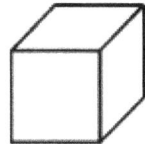

6. Which of the following options shows the number, three greater than the given house number?

   Two hundred seventy three

   (a) 273
   (b) 276
   (c) 275
   (d) 277

7. Look at the given pattern:

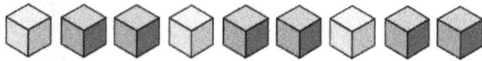

How would you show this pattern using letters?

(a) ABB   (b) ABA

(c) ABC   (d) AAB

8. A fish rod has a code which is used to catch the fish of the same code. Which figure shows the fish, which can be picked by the given fishing rod?

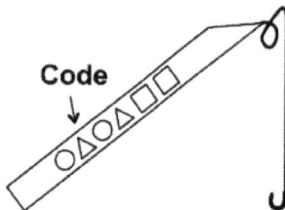

(a)

(b)

(c)

(d)

9. Toothbrush is longer than pin by _____

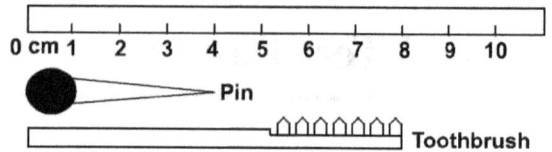

(a) 7 cm   (b) 8 cm

(c) 4 cm   (d) 2 cm

10. Which alphabet belongs to rectangle, circle and triangle?

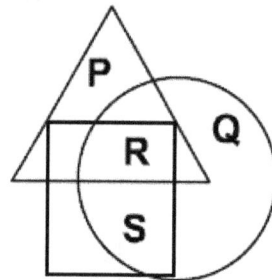

(a) P   (b) Q

(c) R   (d) S

Section II : Mathematical Reasoning

11. Four friends have some playing cards.

Shraddha has a card 2 and said I have an even number.

Golu has a card 3 and said I have an even number.

Ankit has a card 4 and said I have an odd number.

Sheetal has a card 5 and said I have an even number.

Who is right?

(a) Shraddha   (b) Golu

(c) Ankit   (d) Sheetal

12. In a race a student who completes the race in minimum time is the winner. Given below is the time taken by four students W, X , Y and Z to complete a race. Who is the winner?

X: 2 Mins   Y: 180 Sec
Z: 2 Mins 30 Sec   W: 210 Sec

(a) W   (b) X
(c) Y   (d) Z

13. Three friends M, N and O are sitting together. M is taller than N and N is taller than O. Who is the tallest?
(a) M   (b) N
(c) O   (d) Cannot say

14. The numbers that have 2,4,6,8 and 0 in the one's place are called even numbers. Using the information given above find which of the following is even?
(a) 2456   (b) 2520
(c) 7858   (d) All of these

15. Find the position of  in the grid.

(a) Bottom left   (b) Centre
(c) Top centre   (d) Left centre

16. Which of the following is the heaviest?
(a) 1 kg cotton
(b) 1 kg wool
(c) 1 kg iron
(d) All are of the same weight

17. Which of the following figures can be made using four matchsticks?
(a) Circle
(b) Triangle
(c) Square
(d) None of these

18. The cost of three items are given below. Who has enough free money to buy all these items?

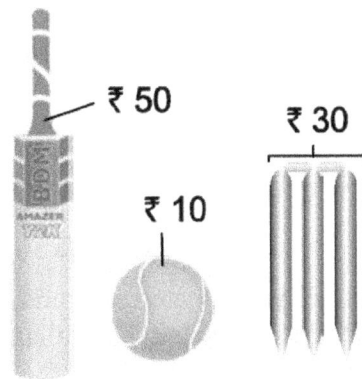

₹ 50   ₹ 30

₹ 10

(a) Golu

(b) Ashu

(c) Mehul

(d) Mohan

19. In a city when temperature reaches 5°C snowfall starts. In which city snowfall is going on?
(a) Jammu : 10°C
(b) Leh : 4°C
(c) Delhi : 14°C
(d) Mumbai : 12°C

20. What temperature is shown by the thermometer?

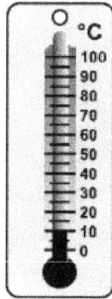

(a) 10°C   (b) 15°C
(c) 20°C   (d) 13°C

Section III : Everyday Mathematics

21. A hotel is 12 meters tall and apartment building is 2 meters taller than the hotel. How many meters tall is the apartment building?
(a) 14 m   (b) 24 m
(c) 20 m   (d) 12 m

22. A shopkeeper bought 340 eggs. Out of them 100 eggs were broken. How many unbroken eggs did the shopkeeper have?
(a) 204   (b) 240
(c) 304   (d) 300

23. Ayush has 5 bunch of bananas. Each bunch has 3 bananas. How many bananas does he have?
(a) 75   (b) 15
(c) 10   (d) 12

24. If a student scoring 8 out of 10 marks gets an A grade, then which among the following will also get an A grade?
(a) 7 out of 10   (b) 5 out of 10
(c) 10 out of 10   (d) 6 out of 10

25. Eight mangoes are shared equally among 2 friends. Each friend will get how many mangoes?
(a) 4   (b) 5
(c) 2   (d) 3

26. I have 10 toffees. I gave two toffees to Priya. I am left with _____ toffees.
(a) 8   (b) 9
(c) 7   (d) 5

27. Ali has 53 marbles. He has 8 more marbles than Henry. If Ali gives 6 marbles to Henry, how many marbles does Henry have now?
(a) 51   (b) 45
(c) 59   (d) 48

28. Mrs. Mehra bought 20 sweets. She wanted her 3 children to share the sweets equally. However, she realised they could not share the sweets equally. What was the greatest number of sweets that each child could receive?
(a) 6   (b) 7
(c) 8   (d) 9

29. Ashu started fixing a broken table at 2:30 p.m. If he took 3 hours 10 minutes to fix the broken table, at what time did he finish?

2.30 p.m.

(a) 6:30 pm   (b) 4:40 pm
(c) 5:30 pm   (d) 5:40 pm

30. Mr. Kapoor had some apples. He gave 13 apples to his son and 16 apples to his daughter. He had 11 apples left. How many apples did he have at first?
   (a) 40   (b) 7
   (c) 14   (d) 28

Section IV : Achievers Section

31. Shraddha measured the height of a table. She also measured the height of a door. The height of the table was 25 cm shorter than the height of the door. If the height of the door was 150 cm, what was the height of the table?
   (a) 125 cm   (b) 175 cm
   (c) 135 cm   (d) 185 cm

32. The weight of Anju and Soni is 93 kg. If the weight of Soni is 31 kg, how much heavier is Anju than Soni?
   (a) 31 kg   (b) 93 kg
   (c) 62 kg   (d) 124 kg

33. Shubhra and Shraddha went shopping and they bought some things. What is the total cost of these things?

   (a) ₹ 130   (b) ₹ 145
   (c) ₹ 185   (d) ₹ 135

34. One morning, Ashu saw that out of 70 birds only 24 were left. The rest had gone away. How many birds had gone away?
   (a) 94   (b) 56
   (c) 64   (d) 46

35. Micky collects sticks from the jungle. He sells them in the market. He uses 14 sticks to make 1 bundle. How many sticks will 6 bundles have?
   (a) 20   (b) 60
   (c) 42   (d) 84

Answer Keys

SECTION 1 : MATHEMATICAL REASONING

1. NUMBERS SENSE

Answer Key									
1. (d)	2. (a)	3. (a)	4. (b)	5. (c)	6. (b)	7. (d)	8. (b)	9. (d)	10. (c)
11. (d)	12. (a)	13. (b)	14. (d)	15. (b)	16. (d)	17. (d)	18. (a)	19. (a)	20. (c)
21. (a)	22. (c)	23. (d)	24. (c)	25. (c)					

HOTS				
1. (c)	2. (d)	3. (d)	4. (a)	5. (c)

2. ADDITION AND SUBTRACTION

Answer Key									
1. (a)	2. (b)	3. (d)	4. (c)	5. (b)	6. (d)	7. (a)	8. (a)	9. (a)	10. (a)
11. (d)	12. (c)	13. (d)	14. (a)	15. (a)	16. (a)	17. (b)	18. (d)	19. (a)	20. (c)
21. (b)	22. (a)	23. (d)	24. (d)	25. (b)					

HOTS				
1. (a)	2. (c)	3. (b)	4. (c)	5. (d)

3. MULTIPLICATION

					Answer Key				
1. (b)	2. (a)	3. (c)	4. (c)	5. (d)	6. (d)	7. (b)	8. (d)	9. (c)	10. (a)
11. (b)	12. (d)	13. (c)	14. (d)	15. (a)	16. (c)	17. (d)	18. (d)	19. (b)	20. (c)
21. (b)	22. (d)	23. (b)	24. (d)	25. (c)					

		HOTS		
1. (b)	2. (a)	3. (a)	4. (b)	5. (b)

4. DIVISION

					Answer Key				
1. (b)	2. (c)	3. (b)	4. (d)	5. (c)	6. (d)	7. (a)	8. (a)	9. (b)	10. (d)
11. (b)	12. (c)	13. (a)	14. (b)	15. (b)	16. (d)	17. (a)	18. (d)	19. (d)	20. (b)
21. (d)	22. (c)	23. (d)	24. (d)	25. (b)					

		HOTS		
1. (d)	2. (c)	3. (c)	4. (d)	5. (a)

5. MEASUREMENT

					Answer Key				
1. (b)	2. (d)	3. (c)	4. (b)	5. (b)	6. (c)	7. (d)	8. (a)	9. (c)	10. (c)
11. (c)	12. (b)	13. (c)	14. (d)	15. (d)	16. (c)	17. (b)	18. (a)	19. (b)	20. (c)
21. (c)	22. (c)	23. (b)	24. (b)	25. (c)					

		HOTS		
1. (b)	2. (a)	3. (c)	4. (c)	5. (b)

6. TIME

Answer Key

1. (d)	2. (b)	3. (a)	4. (a)	5. (a)	6. (b)	7. (d)	8. (a)	9. (c)	10. (c)
11. (a)	12. (b)	13. (d)	14. (d)	15. (a)	16. (b)	17. (b)	18. (a)	19. (a)	20. (a)
21. (b)	22. (c)	23. (c)	24. (b)	25. (d)					

HOTS

1. (b)	2. (c)	3. (b)	4. (a)	5. (d)

7. MONEY

Answer Key

1. (b)	2. (c)	3. (d)	4. (a)	5. (c)	6. (b)	7. (c)	8. (c)	9. (d)	10. (a)
11. (b)	12. (c)	13. (d)	14. (a)	15. (b)	16. (d)	17. (c)	18. (a)	19. (b)	20. (b)
21. (b)	22. (c)	23. (c)	24. (d)	25. (c)					

HOTS

1. (c)	2. (b)	3. (c)	4. (d)	5. (a)

8. GEOMETRICAL SHAPES

Answer Key

1. (b)	2. (d)	3. (a)	4. (c)	5. (d)	6. (a)	7. (d)	8. (c)	9. (a)	10. (a)
11. (b)	12. (b)	13. (a)	14. (a)	15. (a)	16. (a)	17. (a)	18. (a)	19. (b)	20. (a)
21. (a)	22. (b)	23. (c)	24. (b)	25. (d)					

HOTS

1. (c)	2. (a)	3. (b)	4. (c)	5. (b)

9. PICTOGRAPHS

SECTION 2 : LOGICAL REASONING

1. PATTERNS

2. ANALOGY

3. CLASSIFICATION

4. MEASURING UNITS

Answer Key									
1. (b)	2. (a)	3. (d)	4. (b)	5. (c)	6. (c)	7. (c)	8. (c)	9. (a)	10. (c)
11. (b)	12. (a)	13. (b)	14. (c)	15. (b)	16. (c)	17. (a)	18. (b)	19. (c)	20. (b)

5. GEOMETRICAL SHAPES

Answer Key									
1. (b)	2. (c)	3. (b)	4. (c)	5. (a)	6. (b)	7. (c)	8. (c)	9. (d)	10. (b)
11.(b)	12. (c)	13. (a)	14. (a)	15. (b)	16. (c)	17. (a)	18. (c)	19. (c)	20. (a)

6. RANKING TEST

Answer Key									
1. (b)	2. (a)	3. (c)	4. (c)	5. (d)	6. (c)	7. (c)	8. (d)	9. (a)	10. (c)
11.(b)	12. (a)	13. (c)	14. (d)	15. (b)	16. (d)	17. (c)	18. (a)	19. (d)	20. (c)

7. GROUPING OF FIGURES AND EMBEDDED FIGURES

Answer Key									
1. (c)	2. (a)	3. (b)	4. (a)	5.(c)	6. (b)	7. (b)	8. (b)	9. (c)	10. (b)
11. (b)	12. (c)	13. (b)	14. (d)	15. (b)	16. (a)	17. (c)	18. (c)	19. (b)	20. (b)

8. CODING-DECODING

Answer Key									
1. (b)	2. (c)	3. (c)	4. (b)	5. (d)	6. (c)	7. (a)	8. (a)	9. (c)	10. (b)
11. (d)	12. (b)	13. (a)	14. (c)	15. (b)	16. (a)	17. (c)	18. (b)	19. (b)	20. (c)

MODEL TEST PAPER – 1

				Answer Key					
1. (b)	2. (a)	3. (c)	4. (c)	5. (c)	6. (c)	7. (d)	8. (a)	9. (b)	10. (d)
11. (c)	12. (b)	13. (c)	14. (a)	15. (c)	16. (c)	17. (d)	18. (d)	19. (a)	20. (d)
21. (a)	22. (d)	23. (a)	24. (c)	25. (b)	26. (c)	27. (b)	28. (c)	29. (b)	30. (d)
31. (a)	32. (b)	33. (b)	34. (d)	35. (b)					

MODEL TEST PAPER – 2

				Answer Key					
1. (a)	2. (a)	3. (c)	4. (a)	5. (a)	6. (b)	7. (a)	8. (a)	9. (c)	10. (c)
11. (a)	12. (b)	13. (a)	14. (d)	15. (b)	16. (c)	17. (c)	18. (a)	19. (b)	20. (a)
21. (a)	22. (b)	23. (b)	24. (c)	25. (a)	26. (a)	27. (a)	28. (a)	29. (d)	30. (a)
31. (a)	32. (a)	33. (d)	34. (d)	35. (d)					

Appendix

There are different organizations that conduct these examinations and covering all of them is not needed as the focus should be to understand the main type of exams conducted. They are similar for these organizations with the difference being the change in name of the exam.

Science Olympiad Foundation (SOF)		
S. No.	**Name of Exam**	**Grade**
1.	National Science Olympiad (NSO)	Class 1-10
2.	National Cyber Olympiad (NCO)	Class 1-10
3.	International Mathematics Olympiad (IMO)	Class 1-10
4.	International English Olympiad (IEO)	Class 1-10
5.	International Commerce Olympiad (ICO)	Class 1-10
6.	International General Knowledge Olympiad (IGKO)	Class 1-10
7.	International Social Studies Olympiad (ISSO)	Class 1-10
Indian Talent Olympiad (ITO)		
S. No.	**Name of Exam**	**Grade**
1.	International Science Olympiad (ISO)	Class 1-12
2.	International Math Olympiad (IMO)	Class 1-12
3.	English International Olympiad (EIO)	Class 1-12
4.	General Knowledge International Olympiad (GKIO)	Class 1-12
5.	International Computer Olympiad (ICO)	Class 1-12
6.	International Drawing Olympiad (IDO)	Class 1-12
7.	National Essay Olympiad (NESO)	Class 1-12
8.	National Social Studies Olympiad (NSSO)	Class 1-12
EduHeal Foundation		
S. No.	**Name of Exam**	**Grade**
1.	Eduheal International Cyber Olympiad (ICO)	Class 1-12
2.	Eduheal International English Olympiad (IEO)	Class 1-12
3.	National Interactive Math Olympiad (NIMO)	Class 1-12
4.	National Interactive Science Olympiad (NISO)	Class 1-12
5.	International General Knowledge Olympiad (IGO)	Class 1-12
6.	National Space Science Olympiad (NSSO)	Class 1-12

Humming Bird Education

S. No.	Name of Exam	Grade
1.	Humming Bird Commerce Competency Olympiad (HCC)	Class 1-12
2.	Humming Bird Cyber Olympiad (HCO)	Class 1-12
3.	Humming Bird English Olympiad (HEO)	Class 1-12
4.	Humming Bird General Knowledge Olympiad (HGO)	Class 1-12
5.	Humming Bird Hindi Olympiad (HHO)	Class 1-12
6.	Humming Bird Mathematics Olympiad (HMO)	Class 1-12
7.	Humming Bird Science Olympiad (HSO)	Class 1-12
8.	Humming Bird Aptitude and Reasoning Olympiad (ARO)	Class 1-12
9.	Humming Bird Spelling Competition (Spell BEE)	Class 1-12
10.	Humming Bird Language Olympiad	Class 1-12

International Assessments for Indian Schools (IAIS) (MacMillan and EEA Collaboration)

S. No.	Name of Exam	Grade
1.	IAIS Maths Olympiad	Class 3-12
2.	IAIS ScienceOlympiad	Class 3-12
3.	IAIS English Olympiad	Class 3-12
4.	IAIS Digital Technologies Olympiad	Class 3-12

SilverZone Foundation

S. No.	Name of Exam	Grade
1.	International Informatics Olympiad	Class 1-12
2.	International Olympiad of Mathematics	Class 1-12
3.	International Olympiad of Science	Class 1-12

Unified Council

S. No.	Name of Exam	Grade
1.	Unified Council Cyber Exam	Class 1-12
2.	Unified International English Olympiad.	Class 1-12
3.	Unified International Mathematics Olympiad (UIMO)	Class 1-12

Unicus

S. No.	Name of Exam	Grade
1.	Unicus Non-Routine Mathematics Olympiad (UNRMO)	Class 1-11
2.	Unicus Mathematics Olympiad (UMO)	Class 1-11

3.	Unicus Science Olympiad (USO)	Class 1-11
4.	Unicus English Olympiad (UEO)	Class 1-11
5.	Unicus Cyber Olympiad (UCO)	Class 1-11
6.	Unicus General knowledge Olympiad (UGKO)	Class 1-11
7.	Unicus Critical Thinking Olympiad (UCTO)	Class 1-11

CREST (Online Mode)		
S. No.	**Name of Exam**	**Grade**
1.	Mathematics (CMO)	Classes KG-10
2.	Science (CSO)	Classes KG-10
3.	English (CEO)	Classes KG-10
4.	Computer (CCO)	Classes 1-10
5.	Reasoning (CRO)	Classes 1-10
6.	Spell Bee Summer (CSB)	Classes 1-8
7.	Spell Bee Winter (CSBW)	Classes 1-8
8.	Mental Maths (MMO)	Classes 1-12
9.	Green Warrior Olympiad (GWO)	Classes 1-12

How To Apply?

Anyone willing to participate in the Olympiad exam can follow these steps to apply for the exam:

☞ Log in to the official website of the conducting organization.

☞ Find the Registration Option to register

☞ Fill up the details such as Student Name, Parent Name, School Name, Class, Postal Address, E-mail Address, Password, etc.

☞ Select the subjects you want to apply for. Pay the necessary registration fees and you are done.

☞ You will receive necessary details on your email id.

There are no minimum marks required by the Olympiad conducting organizations to apply for the exam.

Awards

Based on the organization rules, students as well as schools participating in these exams are awarded with several recognitions based on the marks they score.

🕐🕐🕐

www.ingramcontent.com/pod-product-compliance
Lightning Source LLC
Chambersburg PA
CBHW080558090426
42735CB00016B/3275